THE EARLY MOTION

ALSO BY JAMES DICKEY

Into the Stone and Other Poems
Drowning With Others
Helmets
Buckdancer's Choice
James Dickey: Poems 1957–1967
Babel to Byzantium
The Eye-Beaters, Blood, Victory, Madness,
    Buckhead and Mercy
Deliverance
Self-Interviews
Sorties
The Zodiac
The Strength of Fields
Falling, May Day Sermon, and Other Poems
Puella

THE
EARLY
MOTION

Drowning with Others
and
Helmets

James Dickey

Wesleyan University Press
MIDDLETOWN, CONNECTICUT

Among the poems in *Drowning with Others* are a number that have previously been printed elsewhere. Grateful acknowledgments are made to *The Atlantic Monthly, Choice, Encounter, Hudson Review, Kenyon Review, Partisan Review, Poetry, Poetry Dial, Quarterly Review of Literature, Sewanee Review, Virginia Quarterly Review,* and *Yale Review;* also to *The New Yorker,* in whose pages the following poems first appeared: "Autumn," "A Birth," "For the Nightly Ascent of the Hunter Orion Over a Forest Clearing," "The Heaven of Animals," "In the Mountain Tent," "In the Tree House at Night," "The Lifeguard," "Listening to Foxhounds," "The Magus," "The Movement of Fish," and "The Salt Marsh."

Most of the poems in *Helmets* were previously published elsewhere. For permission to reprint them, the author is grateful to the editors of *Hudson Review; The Paris Review; The Sewanee Review; The Virginia Quarterly Review; The Yale Review; The New Yorker,* in which the following first appeared: "At Darien Bridge," "The Beholders," "Breath," "Bums, on Waking," "Cherrylog Road," "The Driver," "The Dusk of Horses," "Fence Wire," "Goodbye to Serpents," "The Ice Skin," "Kudzu," "In the Marble Quarry," "The Poisoned Man," "The Scarred Girl," and Part I of "On the Coosawattee"; and *Poetry,* in which the following first appeared: "The Being," "A Folk Singer of the Thirties," and Part II of "On the Coosawattee."

The author would like to thank the editors of *The Virginia Quarterly Review* for the Emily Balch Prize awarded to "Springer Mountain," and the directors of the John Simon Guggenheim Memorial Foundation for the fellowship on which these poems were written.

Manufactured in the United States of America
First edition

Library of Congress Cataloging in Publication Data

Dickey, James.
    The early motion.

    Contents: Drowning with others—Helmets.
    I. Dickey, James. Helmets. 1981. II. Title.
PS3554.I32A6   1981   811'.54   81-15972
ISBN 0-8195-5061-2   AACR2
ISBN 0-8195-6070-7 (pbk.)

To Maxine

light and warmth

This volume brings together all the poems in my first two books published with Wesleyan University Press. The poems are a complete and I hope valuable record of the early phase of my writing life, and represent my attitudes toward the subjects, and toward imagery, rhythm, and form, at the time of writing, roughly from 1959 to 1965.

The themes, which have been expanded and explored in my later work, are in these poems announced and given such treatment as my abilities allowed. These poems emerged from what I call a night-rhythm, something felt in pulse not word. How this anapestic sound was engendered by other poetry, good or bad—by Tennyson, Swinburne, and also by Poe, Kipling, and Robert Service—I cannot say, except to assert that I had read these poets, and I have always liked heavy recurrence of stress. First I heard, then I wrote, and then I began to reason; when I reasoned, I wrote more of the same. The reasoning ran something like this: suppose you have lines like "There's a land where the mountains are nameless, /And the rivers all run God knows where;/There are lives that are erring and aimless,/And deaths that just hang by a hair," and you decide that the level of meaning, compelling as it may be to saloon-keepers and retired postmen, is not good, but that the surge of the rhythm *is*, what then? What if images, insights, metaphors, evaluations, nightmarish narratives, all of originality and true insight, were put into—or *brought* into—the self-generating on-go that seems to have existed before any poem and to continue after any actual poem ends? What if these things were tried? What then might be done? What might become?

On some such assumption, more or less dictated by the blood, by the nerves' hunger for unassailable rhythmic authority, most of these poems were written. At one end of the spectrum of possibility lay the auto-intoxication of Swinburne and Poe, and at the other end the prosaical flatness of William Carlos Williams; these are the obvious but by no means the utter extremes. In the poems of *Drowning With Others* I edged toward the end of sound over sense, toward the foreordained hammering of ultra-rhythmical English, and tried to make the concepts, images, and themes of my life conform to what the night-rhythm had caused to come through me.

The themes that poured into the night-sound were memories of warfare, particularly the air and island combat of the South Pacific, and also (perhaps related in some way) hunting with bow and arrow, which I discovered and began to practice at this time. Also, themes of animals in their alien and instinctive existence, of European travel, which I had first experienced in the mid-fifties, and the continuities of blood and family. I found that although I liked the concentration and single-impact penetration of the short poem, I also liked the expansiveness and opportunity for multi-level development afforded by the long one. In *Drowning With Others* I experimented with poems in several parts, such as "The Owl King," in which a single action is given from three points of view. In *Helmets* I worked toward longer, more inclusive presentations, as in "Approaching Prayer," for example, and in "Drinking from a Helmet," which I considered my most ambitious effort up to that point, I splintered the experience undergone in the poem into nineteen fragments of varying lengths, and by this means tried to get the lyric "timeless-moment" intensity and the enveloping structure of a narrative into the same format. In *Helmets*, though I still relied on the night-rhythm, the sound-before-meaning, I also wanted to give more play to narrative movement, the story-value of what was being said, and consequently I toned down the heavy bombardment of stress and relied more on matter-of-fact statement and declaration; I went toward the flat end of the spectrum, where narrative—or long narrative, anyway—usually lies.

If you add to these elements not only the sound of the folk-guitar, the simple chordal structure of the music I was just beginning to learn when I wrote these poems, together with the ballad-themes often dealt with by Appalachian musicians, you have pretty much what I was about in these two books, or thought I was about, and the principal ways that led to my getting whatever it was I got, may have got, here.

The method of treatment is, I think, consistent, and the emphasis on the rhythmic component of poetry is more salient here than in my later work, a fact that may interest some readers. What I have done subsequently depends in an integral way on these poems; in the "early motion" can also be seen and heard the later motion, and doubtless, when all the poems are done, the whole motion as well.

James Dickey
Columbia, S.C.
April, 1981

CONTENTS

PREFACE   vii

DROWNING WITH OTHERS

❖ PART ONE

THE LIFEGUARD   3
LISTENING TO FOXHOUNDS   6
A DOG SLEEPING ON MY FEET   8
THE MOVEMENT OF FISH   10
THE HEAVEN OF ANIMALS   12
A BIRTH   14
FOG ENVELOPS THE ANIMALS   15
THE SUMMONS   17
IN THE TREE HOUSE AT NIGHT   19
FOR THE NIGHTLY ASCENT OF THE HUNTER ORION
     OVER A FOREST CLEARING   21
THE RIB   23
THE OWL KING   25

❖ PART TWO

BETWEEN TWO PRISONERS   35
ARMOR   38
IN THE LUPANAR AT POMPEII   41
DROWNING WITH OTHERS   44
A VIEW OF FUJIYAMA AFTER THE WAR   46
THE ISLAND   48

❖ PART THREE

DOVER: BELIEVING IN KINGS   51
TO HIS CHILDREN IN DARKNESS   59
A SCREENED PORCH IN THE COUNTRY   62
THE DREAM FLOOD   64
THE SCRATCH   66
HUNTING CIVIL WAR RELICS AT NIMBLEWILL CREEK   68
THE TWIN FALLS   71
THE HOSPITAL WINDOW   72

❖ PART FOUR

THE MAGUS   75
ANTIPOLIS   77
THE CHANGE   79
AUTUMN   80
SNOW ON A SOUTHERN STATE   81
TO LANDRUM GUY, BEGINNING TO WRITE AT SIXTY   84
FACING AFRICA   86
INSIDE THE RIVER   88
THE SALT MARSH   90
IN THE MOUNTAIN TENT   92

HELMETS

❖ PART ONE

THE DUSK OF HORSES	97
FENCE WIRE	99
AT DARIEN BRIDGE	101
CHENILLE	103
ON THE COOSAWATTEE	106
WINTER TROUT	112
SPRINGER MOUNTAIN	115

❖ PART TWO

CHERRYLOG ROAD	119
THE SCARRED GIRL	124
KUDZU	126
THE BEHOLDERS	130
THE POISONED MAN	132
IN THE MARBLE QUARRY	134
A FOLK SINGER OF THE THIRTIES	136

❖ PART THREE

THE BEING   143
BREATH   147
THE ICE SKIN   150
BUMS, ON WAKING   153
GOODBYE TO SERPENTS   156
IN THE CHILD'S NIGHT   159
APPROACHING PRAYER   161

❖ PART FOUR

THE DRIVER   169
HORSES AND PRISONERS   172
DRINKING FROM A HELMET   175

DROWNING WITH OTHERS

PART ONE

THE LIFEGUARD

In a stable of boats I lie still,
From all sleeping children hidden.
The leap of a fish from its shadow
Makes the whole lake instantly tremble.
With my foot on the water, I feel
The moon outside

Take on the utmost of its power.
I rise and go out through the boats.
I set my broad sole upon silver,
On the skin of the sky, on the moonlight,
Stepping outward from earth onto water
In quest of the miracle

This village of children believed
That I could perform as I dived
For one who had sunk from my sight.
I saw his cropped haircut go under.
I leapt, and my steep body flashed
Once, in the sun.

Dark drew all the light from my eyes.
Like a man who explores his death
By the pull of his slow-moving shoulders,
I hung head down in the cold,
Wide-eyed, contained, and alone
Among the weeds,

And my fingertips turned into stone
From clutching immovable blackness.
Time after time I leapt upward
Exploding in breath, and fell back
From the change in the children's faces
At my defeat.

Beneath them I swam to the boathouse
With only my life in my arms
To wait for the lake to shine back
At the risen moon with such power
That my steps on the light of the ripples
Might be sustained.

Beneath me is nothing but brightness
Like the ghost of a snowfield in summer.
As I move toward the center of the lake,
Which is also the center of the moon,
I am thinking of how I may be
The savior of one

Who has already died in my care.
The dark trees fade from around me.
The moon's dust hovers together.
I call softly out, and the child's

Voice answers through blinding water.
Patiently, slowly,

He rises, dilating to break
The surface of stone with his forehead.
He is one I do not remember
Having ever seen in his life.
The ground I stand on is trembling
Upon his smile.

I wash the black mud from my hands.
On a light given off by the grave
I kneel in the quick of the moon
At the heart of a distant forest
And hold in my arms a child
Of water, water, water.

LISTENING TO FOXHOUNDS

When in that gold
Of fires, quietly sitting
With the men whose brothers are hounds,

You hear the first tone
Of a dog on scent, you look from face
To face, to see whose will light up.

When that light comes
Inside the dark light of the fire,
You know which chosen man has heard

A thing like his own dead
Speak out in a marvelous, helpless voice
That he has been straining to hear.

Miles away in the dark,
His enchanted dog can sense
How his features glow like a savior's,

And begins to hunt
In a frenzy of desperate pride.
Among us, no one's eyes give off a light

For the red fox
Playing in and out of his scent,
Leaping stones, doubling back over water.

Who runs with the fox
Must sit here like his own image,
Giving nothing of himself

To the sensitive flames,
With no human joy rising up,
Coming out of his face to be seen.

And it is hard,
When the fox leaps into his burrow,
To keep that singing down,

To sit with the fire
Drawn into one's secret features,
And all eyes turning around

From the dark wood
Until they come, amazed, upon
A face that does not shine

Back from itself,
That holds its own light and takes more,
Like the face of the dead, sitting still,

Giving no sign,
Making no outcry, no matter
Who may be straining to hear.

A DOG SLEEPING ON MY FEET

Being his resting place,
I do not even tense
The muscles of a leg
Or I would seem to be changing.
Instead, I turn the page
Of the notebook, carefully not

Remembering what I have written,
For now, with my feet beneath him
Dying like embers,
The poem is beginning to move
Up through my pine-prickling legs
Out of the night wood,

Taking hold of the pen by my fingers.
Before me the fox floats lightly,
On fire with his holy scent.
All, all are running.
Marvelous is the pursuit,
Like a dazzle of nails through the ankles,

Like a twisting shout through the trees
Sent after the flying fox
Through the holes of logs, over streams
Stock-still with the pressure of moonlight.
My killed legs,
My legs of a dead thing, follow,

Quick as pins, through the forest,
And all rushes on into dark
And ends on the brightness of paper.
When my hand, which speaks in a daze

The hypnotized language of beasts,
Shall falter, and fail

Back into the human tongue,
And the dog gets up and goes out

To wander the dawning yard,
I shall crawl to my human bed
And lie there smiling at sunrise,
With the scent of the fox

Burning my brain like an incense,
Floating out of the night wood,
Coming home to my wife and my sons
From the dream of an animal,
Assembling the self I must wake to,
Sleeping to grow back my legs.

THE MOVEMENT OF FISH

No water is still, on top.
Without wind, even, it is full
Of a chill, superficial agitation.
It is easy to forget,
Or not to know at all

That fish do not move
By means of this rippling
Along the outside of water, or
By anything touching on air.
Where they are, it is still,

Under a wooden bridge,
Under the poised oar
Of a boat, while the rower leans
And blows his mistaken breath
To make the surface shake,

Or yells at it, or sings,
Half believing the brilliant scan
Of ripples will carry the fish away
On his voice like a buried wind.
Or it may be that a fish

Is simply lying under
The ocean-broad sun
Which comes down onto him
Like a tremendous, suffusing
Open shadow

Of gold, where nothing is,
Sinking into the water,

Becoming dark around
His body. Where he is now
Could be gold mixed

With absolute blackness.
The surface at mid-sea shivers,
But he does not feel it
Like a breath, or like anything.
Yet suddenly his frame shakes,

Convulses the whole ocean
Under the trivial, quivering
Surface, and he is,
Hundreds of feet away,
Still picking up speed, still shooting

Through half-gold,
Going nowhere. Nothing sees him.
One must think of this to understand
The instinct of fear and trembling,
And, of its one movement, the depth.

THE HEAVEN OF ANIMALS

Here they are. The soft eyes open.
If they have lived in a wood
It is a wood.
If they have lived on plains
It is grass rolling
Under their feet forever.

Having no souls, they have come,
Anyway, beyond their knowing.
Their instincts wholly bloom
And they rise.
The soft eyes open.

To match them, the landscape flowers,
Outdoing, desperately
Outdoing what is required:
The richest wood,
The deepest field.

For some of these,
It could not be the place
It is, without blood.
These hunt, as they have done,
But with claws and teeth grown perfect,

More deadly than they can believe.
They stalk more silently,
And crouch on the limbs of trees,
And their descent
Upon the bright backs of their prey

May take years
In a sovereign floating of joy.
And those that are hunted
Know this as their life,
Their reward: to walk

Under such trees in full knowledge
Of what is in glory above them,
And to feel no fear,
But acceptance, compliance.
Fulfilling themselves without pain

At the cycle's center,
They tremble, they walk
Under the tree,
They fall, they are torn,
They rise, they walk again.

A BIRTH

Inventing a story with grass,
I find a young horse deep inside it.
I cannot nail wires around him;
My fence posts fail to be solid,

And he is free, strangely, without me.
With his head still browsing the greenness,
He walks slowly out of the pasture
To enter the sun of his story.

My mind freed of its own creature,
I find myself deep in my life
In a room with my child and my mother,
When I feel the sun climbing my shoulder

Change, to include a new horse.

14

FOG ENVELOPS THE ANIMALS

Fog envelops the animals.
Not one can be seen, and they live.
At my knees, a cloud wears slowly
Up out of the buried earth.
In a white suit I stand waiting.

Soundlessly whiteness is eating
My visible self alive.
I shall enter this world like the dead,
Floating through tree trunks on currents
And streams of untouchable pureness

That shine without thinking of light.
My hands burn away at my sides
In the pale, risen ghosts of deep rivers.
In my hood peaked like a flame,
I feel my own long-hidden,

Long-sought invisibility
Come forth from my solid body.
I stand with all beasts in a cloud.
Of them I am deadly aware,
And they not of me, in this life.

Only my front teeth are showing
As the dry fog mounts to my lips
In a motion long buried in water,
And now, one by one, my teeth
Like rows of candles go out.

In the spirit of flame, my hood
Holds the face of my soul without burning,
And I drift forward
Through the hearts of the curdling oak trees,
Borne by the river of Heaven.

My arrows, keener than snowflakes,
Are with me whenever I touch them.
Above my head, the trees exchange their arms
In the purest fear upon earth.
Silence. Whiteness. Hunting.

THE SUMMONS

For something out of sight,
I cup a grass-blade in my hands,
Tasting the root, and blow.
I speak to the wind, and it lives.
No hunter has taught me this call;
It comes out of childhood and playgrounds.
I hang my longbow on a branch.
The wind at my feet extends

Quickly out, across the lake,
Containing the sound I have made.
The water below me becomes
Bright ploughland in its body.
I breathe on my thumbs, and am blowing
A horn that encircles the forest.
Across the lake, a tree
Now thrums in tremendous cadence.

Beneath it, some being stumbles,
And answers me slowly and greatly
With a tongue as rasping as sawgrass.
I lower my hands, and I listen
To the beast that shall die of its love.
I sound my green trumpet again,
And the whole wood sings in my palms.
The vast trees are tuned to my bowstring

And the deep-rooted voice I have summoned.
I have carried it here from a playground
Where I rolled in the grass with my brothers.
Nothing moves, but something intends to.
The water that puffed like a wing

Is one flattened blaze through the branches.
Something falls from the bank, and is swimming.
My voice turns around me like foliage,

And I pluck my longbow off the limb
Where it shines with a musical light,
And crouch within death, awaiting
The beast in the water, in love
With the palest and gentlest of children,
Whom the years have turned deadly with knowledge:
Who summons him forth, and now
Pulls wide the great, thoughtful arrow.

IN THE TREE HOUSE AT NIGHT

And now the green household is dark.
The half-moon completely is shining
On the earth-lighted tops of the trees.
To be dead, a house must be still.
The floor and the walls wave me slowly;
I am deep in them over my head.
The needles and pine cones about me

Are full of small birds at their roundest,
Their fists without mercy gripping
Hard down through the tree to the roots
To sing back at light when they feel it.
We lie here like angels in bodies,
My brothers and I, one dead,
The other asleep from much living,

In mid-air huddled beside me.
Dark climbed to us here as we climbed
Up the nails I have hammered all day
Through the sprained, comic rungs of the ladder
Of broom handles, crate slats, and laths
Foot by foot up the trunk to the branches
Where we came out at last over lakes

Of leaves, of fields disencumbered of earth
That move with the moves of the spirit.
Each nail that sustains us I set here;
Each nail in the house is now steadied
By my dead brother's huge, freckled hand.
Through the years, he has pointed his hammer
Up into these limbs, and told us

That we must ascend, and all lie here.
Step after step he has brought me,
Embracing the trunk as his body,
Shaking its limbs with my heartbeat,
Till the pine cones danced without wind
And fell from the branches like apples.
In the arm-slender forks of our dwelling

I breathe my live brother's light hair.
The blanket around us becomes
As solid as stone, and it sways.
With all my heart, I close
The blue, timeless eye of my mind.
Wind springs, as my dead brother smiles
And touches the tree at the root;

A shudder of joy runs up
The trunk; the needles tingle;
One bird uncontrollably cries.
The wind changes round, and I stir
Within another's life. Whose life?
Who is dead? Whose presence is living?
When may I fall strangely to earth,

Who am nailed to this branch by a spirit?
Can two bodies make up a third?
To sing, must I feel the world's light?
My green, graceful bones fill the air
With sleeping birds. Alone, alone
And with them I move gently.
I move at the heart of the world.

FOR THE NIGHTLY ASCENT OF THE HUNTER ORION
OVER A FOREST CLEARING

Now secretness dies of the open.
Yet all around, all over, night
Things are waking fast,
Waking with all their power.
Who can arise

From his dilating shadow
When one foot is longing to tiptoe
And the other to take the live
Stand of a tree that belongs here?
As the owl's gaze

Most slowly begins to create
Its sight from the death of the sun,
As the mouse feels the whole wood turn
The gold of the owl's new eyes,
And the fox moves

Out of the ground where he sleeps,
No man can stand upright
And drag his body forth
Through an open space in the foliage
Unless he rises

As does the hunter Orion,
Thinking to cross a blue hollow
Through the dangers of twilight,
Feeling that he must run
And that he will

Take root forever and stand,
Does both at once, and neither,
Grows blind, and then sees everything,
Steps and becomes a man
Of stars instead,

Who from invisibility
Has come, arranged in the light
Of himself, revealed tremendously
In his fabulous, rigid, eternal
Unlooked-for role.

THE RIB

Something has left itself scattered
Under a bush in the evening,
Not recalling what lay down at first
To make its claimed body for years
Disappear into air,

Or lay with its small bones desiring
To come slowly forth into twilight
Where the moon begins to raise up
A dead tree now at my side.
I pick up a rib

And something like what must be
The bite small animals die of
Encircles myself and the tree,
Coming round again, coming closer,
A breath forming teeth,

Warming the bones of my wrist.
That my radiant palm is unopened,
That my breast is still whole
When I feel it seized on and thrown down
By the madness of hunting

Is a miracle, like the dead moon
Creating black trees with stone fire.
Can it be that the wounds of beasts,
The hurts they inherit no words for,
Are like the mouths

Of holy beings we think of,
So strongly do they breathe upon us

Their bloodletting silence?
A rib in my right side speaks
To me more softly

Than Eve—the bidden, unfreeable shape
Of my own unfinished desire
For life, for death and the Other—
So that the wound in the air
And its giver

Far off in the brush, all teeth,
Hear me answer the patient world
Of love in my side imprisoned
As I rise, going moonward toward better
And better sleep.

THE OWL KING

I. *The Call*

Through the trees, with the moon underfoot,
More soft than I can, I call.
I hear the king of the owls sing
Where he moves with my son in the gloom.
My tongue floats off in the darkness.
I feel the deep dead turn
My blind child round toward my calling,
Through the trees, with the moon underfoot,

In a sound I cannot remember.
It whispers like straw in my ear,
And shakes like a stone under water.
My bones stand on tiptoe inside it.
Which part of the sound did I utter?
Is it song, or is half of it whistling?
What spirit has swallowed my tongue?
Or is it a sound I remember?

And yet it is coming back,
Having gone, adrift on its spirit,
Down, over and under the river,
And stood in a ring in a meadow
Round a child with a bird gravely dancing.
I hear the king of the owls sing.
I did not awaken that sound,
And yet it is coming back,

In touching every tree upon the hill.
The breath falls out of my voice,
And yet the singing keeps on.

The owls are dancing, fastened by their toes
Upon the pines. Come, son, and find me here,
In love with the sound of my voice.
Come calling the same soft song,
And touching every tree upon the hill.

II. *The Owl King*

I swore to myself I would see
When all but my seeing had failed.
Every light was too feeble to show
My world as I knew it must be.
At the top of the staring night
I sat on the oak in my shape
With my claws growing deep into wood
And my sight going slowly out
Inch by inch, as into a stone,
Disclosing the rabbits running
Beneath my bent, growing throne,
And the foxes lighting their hair,
And the serpent taking the shape
Of the stream of life as it slept.
When I thought of the floating sound
In which my wings would outspread,
I felt the hooked tufts on my head
Enlarge, and dream like a crown,
And my voice unplaceable grow
Like a feathery sigh;
I could not place it myself.
For years I humped on the tree
Whose leaves held the sun and the moon.
At last I opened my eyes

In the sun, and saw nothing there.
That night I parted my lids
Once more, and saw dark burn
Greater than sunlight or moonlight,
For it burned from deep within me.
The still wood glowed like a brain.
I prised up my claws, and spread
My huge, ashen wings from my body,
For I heard what I listened to hear.
Someone spoke to me out of the distance
In a voice like my own, but softer.
I rose like the moon from the branch.

Through trees at his light touch trembling
The blind child drifted to meet me,
His blue eyes shining like mine.
In a ragged clearing he stopped,
And I circled, beating above him,
Then fell to the ground and hopped
Forward, taking his hand in my claw.
Every tree's life lived in his fingers.
Gravely we trod with each other
As beasts at their own wedding, dance.
Through the forest, the questioning voice
Of his father came to us there,
As though the one voice of us both,
Its high, frightened sound becoming
A perfect, irrelevant music
In which we profoundly moved,
I in the innermost shining
Of my blazing, invented eyes,
And he in the total of dark.

Each night, now, high on the oak,
With his father calling like music,
He sits with me here on the bough,
His eyes inch by inch going forward
Through stone dark, burning and picking
The creatures out one by one,
Each waiting alive in its own
Peculiar light to be found:
The mouse in its bundle of terror,
The fox in the flame of its hair,
And the snake in the form of all life.
Each night he returns to his bed,
To the voice of his singing father,
To dream of the owl king sitting
Alone in the crown of my will.
In my ruling passion, he rests.
All dark shall come to light.

III. *The Blind Child's Story*

I am playing going down
In my weight lightly,
Down, down the hill.
No one calls me
Out of the air.
The heat is falling
On the backs of my hands
And holding coldness.
They say it shines two ways.
The darkness is great
And luminous in my eyes.
Down I am quickly going;

A leaf falls on me,
It must be a leaf I hear it
Be thin against me, and now
The ground is level,
It moves it is not ground,
My feet flow cold
And wet, and water rushes
Past as I climb out.
I am there, on the other side.
I own the entire world.

It closes a little; the sky
Must be cold, must be giving off
Creatures that stand here.
I say they shine one way.
Trees they are trees around me,
Leaves branches and bark;
I can touch them all; I move
From one to another—someone said
I seem to be blessing them.
I am blessing them
Slowly, one after another
Deeper into the wood.

The dark is changing,
Its living is packed in closer
Overhead—more trees and leaves—
Tremendous. It touches
Something touches my hand,
Smelling it, a cold nose
Of breath, an ear of silk
Is gone. It is here I begin

To call to something unearthly.
Something is here, something before
Me sitting above me
In the wood in a crown,
Its eyes newborn in its head
From the death of the sun.
I can hear it rising on wings.
I hear that fluttering
Cease, and become
Pure soundless dancing
Like leaves not leaves;
Now down out of air
It lumbers to meet me,
Stepping oddly on earth,
Awkwardly, royally.
My father is calling

Through the touched trees;
All distance is weeping and singing.
In my hand I feel
A talon, a grandfather's claw
Bone cold and straining
To keep from breaking my skin.
I know this step, I know it,
And we are deep inside.
My father's voice is over
And under us, sighing.
Nothing is strange where we are.
The huge bird bows and returns,
For I, too, have done the same
As he leads me, rustling,
A pile of leaves in my hands;

The dry feathers shuffle like cards
On his dusty shoulders,
Not touching a tree,
Not brushing the side of a leaf
Or a point of grass.

We stop and stand like bushes.
But my father's music comes
In, goes on, comes in,
Into the wood,
Into the ceased dance.
And now the hard beak whispers
Softly, and we climb
Some steps of bark
Living and climbing with us
Into the leaves.
I sit among leaves,
And the whole branch hums
With the owl's full, weightless power
As he closes his feet on the wood.
My own feet dangle
And tingle down;
My head is pointing
Deep into moonlight,
Deep into branches and leaves,
Directing my blackness there,
The personal dark of my sight,
And now it is turning a color.
My eyes are blue at last.

Something within the place
I look is piled and coiled.

It lifts its head from itself.
Its form is lit, and gives back
What my eyes are giving it freely.
I learn from the master of sight
What to do when the sun is dead,
How to make the great darkness work
As it wants of itself to work.
I feel the tree where we sit
Grow under me, and live.
I may have been here for years;
In the coil, the heaped-up creature
May have taken that long to lift
His head, to break his tongue
From his thin lips,
But he is there. I shut my eyes
And my eyes are gold,
As gold as an owl's,
As gold as a king's.
I open them. Farther off,
Beyond the swaying serpent,
A creature is burning itself
In a smoke of hair through the bushes.
The fox moves; a small thing
Being caught, cries out,
And I understand
How beings and sounds go together;
I understand
The voice of my singing father.
I shall be king of the wood.

Our double throne shall grow
Forever, until I see

The self of every substance
As it crouches, hidden and free.
The owl's face runs with tears
As I take him in my arms
In the glow of original light
Of Heaven. I go down
In my weight lightly down
The tree, and now
Through the soul of the wood
I walk in consuming glory
Past the snake, the fox, and the mouse:
I see as the owl king sees,
By going in deeper than darkness.
The wood comes back in a light
It did not know it withheld,
And I can tell
By its breathing glow
Each tree on which I laid
My hands when I was blind.

I cross the cold-footed flowing,
The creek, a religious fire
Streaming my ankles away,
And climb through the slanted meadow.
My father cannot remember
That he ever lived in this house.
To himself he bays like a hound,
Entranced by the endless beauty
Of his grief-stricken singing and calling.
He is singing simply to moonlight,
Like a dog howling,
And it is holy song

Out of his mouth.
Father, I am coming,
I am here on my own;
I move as you sing,
As if it were Heaven.
It is Heaven. I am walking
To you and seeing
Where I walk home.
What I have touched, I see
With the dark of my blue eyes.
Far off, the owl king
Sings like my father, growing
In power. Father, I touch
Your face. I have not seen
My own, but it is yours.
I come, I advance,
I believe everything, I am here.

PART TWO

BETWEEN TWO PRISONERS

I would not wish to sit
In my shape bound together with wire,
Wedged into a child's sprained desk
In the schoolhouse under the palm tree.
Only those who did could have done it.

One bled from a cut on his temple,
And sat with his yellow head bowed,
His wound for him painfully thinking.
A belief in words grew upon them
That the unbound, who walk, cannot know.

The guard at the window leaned close
In a movement he took from the palm tree,
To hear, in a foreign tongue,
All things which cannot be said.
In the splintering clapboard room

They rested the sides of their faces
On the tops of the desks as they talked.

Because of the presence of children
In the deep signs carved in the desk tops,
Signs on the empty blackboard

Began, like a rain, to appear.
In the luminous chalks of all colors,
Green face, yellow breast, white sails
Whose wing feathers made the wall burn
Like a waterfall seen in a fever,

An angel came boldly to light
From his hands casting green, ragged bolts
Each having the shape of a palm leaf.
Also traced upon darkness in chalk
Was the guard at the rear window leaning

Through the red, vital strokes of his tears.
Behind him, men lying with swords
As with women, heard themselves sing,
And woke, then, terribly knowing
That they were a death squad, singing

In its sleep, in the middle of a war.
A wind sprang out of the tree.
The guard awoke by the window,
And found he had talked to himself
All night, in two voices, of Heaven.

He stood in the sunlit playground
Where the quiet boys knelt together
In their bloodletting trusses of wire,

And saw their mussed, severed heads
Make the ground jump up like a dog.

I watched the small guard be hanged
A year later, to the day,
In a closed horse stall in Manila.
No one knows what language he spoke
As his face changed into all colors,

And gave off his red, promised tears,
Or if he learned blindly to read
A child's deep, hacked hieroglyphics
Which can call up an angel from nothing,
Or what was said for an instant, there,

In the tied, scribbled dark, between him
And a figure drawn hugely in chalk,
Speaking words that can never be spoken
Except in a foreign tongue,
In the end, at the end of a war.

ARMOR

When this is the thing you put on
The world is pieced slowly together
In the power of the crab and the insect.
The make of the eyeball changes
As over your mouth you draw down
A bird's bill made for a man.

As your weight upon earth is redoubled
There is no way of standing alone
More, or no way of being
More with the bound, shining dead.
You have put on what you should wear,
Not into the rattling of battle,

But into a silence where nothing
Threatens but Place itself: the shade
Of the forest, the strange, crowned
Motionless sunlight of Heaven,
With the redbird blinking and shooting
Across the nailed beam of the eyepiece.

In that light, in the wood, in armor,
I look in myself for the being
I was in a life before life
In a glade more silent than breathing,
Where I took off my body of metal
Like a brother whose features I knew

By the feel of their strength on my face
And whose limbs by the shining of mine.
In a vision I fasten him there,
The bright locust shell of my strength

Like a hanged man waiting in Heaven,
And then steal off to my life.

In my home, a night nearer death,
I wake with no shield on my breastbone,
Breathing deep through my sides like an insect,
My closed hand falling and rising
Where it lies like the dead on my heart.
I cannot remember my brother;

Before I was born he went from me
Ablaze with the meaning of typhoid.
In a fever I see him turn slowly
Under the strange, perfect branches
Where somehow I left him to wait
That I might be naked on earth,

His crowned face dazzlingly closed,
His curving limbs giving off
Pure energy into the leaves.
When I give up my hold on my breath
I long to dress deeply at last
In the gold of my waiting brother

Who shall wake and shine on my limbs
As I walk, made whole, into Heaven.
I shall not remember his face
Or my dazed, eternal one
Until I have opened my hand
And touched the grave glow of his breast

To stop the gaunt turning of metal:
Until I have let the still sun
Down into the stare of the eyepiece
And raised its bird's beak to confront
What man is within to live with me
When I begin living forever.

IN THE LUPANAR AT POMPEII

There are tracks which belong to wheels
Long since turned to air and time.
Those are the powerful chariots
I follow down cobblestones,
Not being dragged, exactly,
But not of my own will, either,
Going past the flower sellers'
And the cindery produce market
And the rich man's home, and the house
Of the man who kept a dog
Set in mosaic.

As tourist, but mostly as lecher,
I seek out the dwelling of women
Who all expect me, still, because
They expect anybody who comes.
I am ready to pay, and I do,
And then go in among them
Where on the dark walls of their home
They hold their eternal postures,
Doing badly drawn, exacting,
Too-willing, wide-eyed things
With dry-eyed art.

I sit down in one of the rooms
Where it happened again and again.
I could be in prison, or dead,
Cast down for my sins in a cell
Still filled with a terrible motion
Like the heaving and sighing of earth
To be free of the heat it restrains.
I feel in my heart how the heart

Of the mountain broke, and the women
Fled onto the damp of the walls
And shaped their embraces

To include whoever would come here
After the stone-cutting chariots.
I think of the marvel of lust
Which can always, at any moment,
Become more than it believed,
And almost always is less:
I think of its possible passing
Beyond, into tender awareness,
Into helplessness, weeping, and death:
It must be like the first
Soft floating of ash,

When, in the world's frankest hands,
Someone lay with his body shaken
Free of the self: that amazement—
For we who must try to explain
Ourselves in the house of this flesh
Never can tell the quick heat
Of our own from another's breathing,
Nor yet from the floating of feathers
That form in our lungs when the mountain
Settles like odd, warm snow against
Our willing limbs.

We never can really tell
Whether nature condemns us or loves us
As we lie here dying of breath
And the painted, unchanging women,

Believing the desperate dead
Where they stripped to the skin of the soul
And whispered to us, as to
Their panting, observing selves:
"Passion. Before we die
Let us hope for no longer
But truly know it."

DROWNING WITH OTHERS

There are moments a man turns from us
Whom we have all known until now.
Upgathered, we watch him grow,
Unshipping his shoulder bones

Like human, everyday wings
That he has not ever used,
Releasing his hair from his brain,
A kingfisher's crest, confused

By the God-tilted light of Heaven.
His deep, window-watching smile
Comes closely upon us in waves,
And spreads, and now we are

At last within it, dancing.
Slowly we turn and shine
Upon what is holding us,
As under our feet he soars,

Struck dumb as the angel of Eden,
In wide, eye-opening rings.
Yet the hand on my shoulder fears
To feel my own wingblades spring,

To feel me sink slowly away
In my hair turned loose like a thought
Of a fisherbird dying in flight.
If I opened my arms, I could hear

Every shell in the sea find the word
It has tried to put into my mouth.

Broad flight would become of my dancing,
And I would obsess the whole sea,

But I keep rising and singing
With my last breath. Upon my back,
With his hand on my unborn wing,
A man rests easy as sunlight

Who has kept himself free of the forms
Of the deaf, down-soaring dead,
And me laid out and alive
For nothing at all, in his arms.

A VIEW OF FUJIYAMA AFTER THE WAR

Wind, and all the midges in the air,
On wings you cannot see, awake
Where they must have been sleeping in flight.
I breathe, and twenty miles away

Snow streams from the mountain top
And all other mountains are nothing.
The ground of the enemy's country
Shakes; my bones settle back where they stand.

Through the bloom of gnats in the sun,
Shaken less than my heart by the tremor,
The blossom of a cherry tree appears.
The mountain returns my last breath,

And my hair blows, weightless as snow.
When it is still, when it is as still as this,
It could be a country where no one
Ever has died but of love.

I take the snow's breath and I speak it.
What I say has the form of a flame
Going all through the gnats like their spirit,
And for a swarming moment they become,

Almost, my own drunk face in the air
Against the one mountain in Heaven.
It is better to wait here quietly,
Not for my face to take flight,

But for someone to come from the dead
Other side of the war to this place:

Who thinks of this ground as his home,
Who thinks no one else can be here,

And that no one can see him pass
His hand through a visage of insects,
His hand through the cone of the mountain
To pluck the flower. But will he feel

His sobbing be dug like a wellspring
Or a deep water grow from his lids
To light, and break up the mountain
Which sends his last breath from its summit

As it dances together again?
Can he know that to live at the heart
Of his saved, shaken life, is to stand
Overcome by the enemy's peace?

THE ISLAND

A light come from my head
Showed how to give birth to the dead
That they might nourish me.
In a wink of the blinding sea
I woke through the eyes, and beheld
No change, but what had been,
And what cannot be seen
Any place but a burnt-out war:
The engines, the wheels, and the gear
That bring good men to their backs
Nailed down into wooden blocks,
With the sun on their faces through sand,
And polyps a-building the land
Around them of senseless stone.
The coral and I understood
That these could come to no good
Without the care I could give,
And that I, by them, must live.
I clasped every thought in my head
That bloomed from the magical dead,
And seizing a shovel and rake,
Went out by the ocean to take
My own sweet time, and start
To set a dead army apart.
I hammered the coffins together
Of patience and hobnails and lumber,
And gave them names, and hacked
Deep holes where they were stacked.
Each wooden body, I took
In my arms, and singingly shook
With its being, which stood for my own
More and more, as I laid it down.

At the grave's crude, dazzling verge
My true self strained to emerge
From all they could not save
And did not know they could give.
I buried them where they lay
In the brass-bound heat of the day,
A whole army lying down
In animal-lifted sand.
And then with rake and spade
I curried each place I had stood
On their chests and on their faces,
And planted the rows of crosses
Inside the blue wind of the shore.
I hauled more wood to that ground
And a white fence put around
The soldiers lying in waves
In my life-giving graves.
And a painless joy came to me
When the troopships took to the sea,
And left the changed stone free
Of all but my image and me:
Of the tonsured and perilous green
With its great, delighted design
Of utter finality,
Whose glowing workman stood
In the intricate, knee-high wood
In the midst of the sea's blind leagues,
Kicked off his old fatigues,
Saluted the graves by their rank,
Paraded, lamented, and sank
Into the intelligent light,
And danced, unimagined and free,
Like the sun taking place on the sea.

PART THREE

DOVER: BELIEVING IN KINGS

As we drove down the ramp from the boat
The sun flashed once
Or through hand-shieldedly twice;
In a silence out of a sound
We watched for channel swimmers dim with grease,
Come, here, to the ale of the shallows.
Within a wind, a wind sprang slowly up.
Birds hovered where they were.
As they were there, the airstream of the cliffs
Overcame, came over them
In the sackcloth and breast-beating gray
The king wears newly, at evening.
In a movement you cannot imagine
Of air, the gulls fall, shaken.

No stronger than the teeth in my head
Or a word laid bare
On chilling glass, the breathed stone over us rode.
From its top, the eye may sail,
Outgrowing the graven nerves
Of the brow's long-thought-out lines,

To France, on its own color.
From a child's tall book, I knew this place
The child must believe, with the king:
Where, doubtless, now, lay lovers
Restrained by a cloud, and the moon
Into force coming justly, above.
In a movement you cannot imagine
Of love, the gulls fall, mating.

We stopped; the birds hung up their arms
Inside the wind
So that they heeled; above, around us,
Their harp-strung feathers made
The sound, quickly mortal, of sighing.
We watched them in pure obsession.
Where they did move, we moved
Along the cliffs, the promenade,
The walls, the pebble beach,
And felt the inmost island turn,
In their cross-cut, wing-walking cries,
To a thing, as weeping, sensitive,
And haunted by the balancement of light
The king wears newly, in singing.

We wandered off from the car
In the light, half-sun,
Half-moon, in a worn-down shine out of stone,
And the taste of an iron ladle on the wind.
In the moon's grimed, thumbprint silver
The anchor spoke through the bell,
Far out, the hour that hung in the sea.
I threw a slow-flying stone; it dropped

Inside the brilliant echo of a light.
In a great, clustered, overdrawn sigh
The gulls went up, on a raiment of wings
The king wears newly, in panic.
In a movement you cannot imagine
Of error, the gulls rise, wholly.

We climbed a wall they had flown.
Each light below
On water, shook like a thing in a lathe.
In the heron crest of a lamp,
Among lights, in their treading motion,
The head of my reflection seemed to sing
A dark, quickened side of the truth.
I touched my wife. I saw my son, unborn,
Left living after me, and my Self,
There, freed of myself,
In a stricken shade dancing together,
As a wave rolled under the water,
Lifted and rode in our shadows
The king wears newly, redoubling.

Where we went in, all power failed the house.
I spooned out light
Upon a candle thread. My wife lay down.
Through the flaming, white-bread nerve
I peered from the eye of the mind.
No child from the windowed dark came forth
To the hand, in its pure-blooded fire,
But the basket glow of the crown.
The glass fetched white to a breath; I understood
How the crown must come from within:

Of water made, and a wheel,
And of the things in flame that seems to pant.
In a movement you cannot imagine
Of mirrors, the gulls fall, hidden.

I lay in bed. One hand in its sleeve
Lay open, on my breath.
My shadow, laid stilly beneath me,
Rose, through my form. I heard the bell,
In mist, step backwardly onto the waves.
The wind fell off, as candle shade
Unraveled our walls like knitting, and I,
Undone, outstretched through the trampled shining
Of thousands of miles of the moon,
And the fallen king
Breathed like a nosebleed, there,
Two men wear newly, in hiding.
In a movement you cannot imagine
Of bloodshed, the gulls fall, inward.

I listened for the coming of a barge.
In a cat's-cradling motion
Of oars, my father rocked, in the mist. He died;
He was dying. His whisper fell,
As I, beneath the grave. Below the drowned
I breathed, in the pig-iron taste of my beard.
I yelled, as out of a bucket,
Through my fettered mask, before the dawn
When my arms, my big-footed legs would hang
From pothooks, strange and untimely.
The stone beat like a gull; my father's voice
Came to life, in words, in my ear.

In a movement you cannot imagine
Of prison, the gulls turn, calling.

Believing, then, astoundedly, in a son,
I drew from tufted stone
My sword. I slew my murderer, Lightborn, on the stair:
With the flat of steel, I flashed
Him dead, through his eyes high-piled in the hood.
When the tide came in, I rose
And onto the curded dark climbed out.
In the cliffs, where creatures about me swam,
In their thin, slain, time-serving bones,
The heavy page, the animal print of the chalk,
With wounds I glittered, dazzling as a fish.
In my short-horned, wool-gathering crown
I came from the beasts to the kingdoms
The king wears newly, in passing.

The sun fell down, through the moon.
The dead held house.
I hove my father to my back
And climbed from his barrow, there.
Pride helped me pick a queen and get a son.
The heroic drink of the womb
Broke, then, into swanlike song.
One came with scepter, one with cup,
One goatlike back'd, and one with the head of a god.
My mask fell away, and my gyves.
Through my sons I leapt in my ghost
The king wears newly, on fire.
In a movement you cannot imagine
Of birth, the gulls fall, crying.

55

In the cloudlike, packed, and layered realm
I wept, when I would sing.
I laid my father down where he must lie,
And entered, again, in my passion,
An older, incredible shape
Becoming young, as the cliffs let fall within stone
Their shadow green down from the crest.
I stood on the cliff top, alone.
My father's body in my heart
Like a buried candle danced. I saw it shed on the sea,
On the flats of water, far out:
A rough, selected brightness
Exchanging a flame for a wheel
The king wears slowly, in measure.

Birds drifted in my breath as it was drawn
From the stressing glitter
Of water. Where France becomes
Another blue lid for the eye,
I felt my green eyes turn
Surprisingly blue, of one great look upon distance.
The sword dissolved, in my hands; wings beat.
I watched them rise from my arms, and stood
Excited forever by love. I saw the child's eye shine
From his book, a wave of justified light.
The prison like organs moaned. In a death like life
I sang like a head on a pole.
In a movement you cannot imagine
Of emblems, the gulls fall, silent.

One foot shone to me, from the sun.
I felt the sun's

Mortality increase. In the blown,
Brow-beating light, I woke, and saw the room
Arise like a yeast from the floor,
The window come down like a bee.
In the long-legged, warm-bodied bed
I thought of him who would tell
To himself, gotten-up in his candle-cast bones:
Every man, every man
Not a king. It is I
The king wears newly, in lasting.
In a movement you cannot imagine
Of spells, the gulls fall, listening.

How shall the stranger wake
Who has issued from dark
With the king? With gulls asleep
In the blue-burning grass? And on the sea,
A blaze that is counting itself,
The white birds holding
Still, on the field of the cloth of gold,
On the self and soul of the air?
Who stands, big-footed with glory, yet,
With the sound falling out of his voice
And his voice halfway to his son
Whose breath Time holds, in a woman?
In a movement you cannot imagine
Of silence, the gulls fall, waiting.

Why not as a prince, who, as
From a distance, wakes?
Who turns from the regular mirror
To watch, at the flawing pane,

Pale fire on a hairspring still burning
In the puddled socket, and the fishing flash
On the shuffled rock of a wave
Overturn, in an inlaid crash
In the window's half-mirror, half-air
As he steps through this room from the sea?
A tossed, green crown on his head,
He combs down the hair of his spirit,
Which is dead, but for the eyes
The king wears newly, at thirty:

Yet who is *he?* Whom does he face, in reflection?
The stained-glass king,
Or the child, grown tall, who cried to earth and air,
To books and water: to sun and father and fire
And nothingness to come and crown him, here?
Or are they, both of them, and neither,
This straw-headed knave, in blue-printed blue jeans appearing:
Who, in exultant tenderness upon a woman's sleep
Onlooks, then leaps out the door, out of that
Up onto the seaside path, and when the sheep track dies,
Two late and idle lovers in the grass
Kicks into love, and goes up the cliffs to be crowned?
In a movement you cannot imagine
Of England, the king smiles, climbing: running.

TO HIS CHILDREN IN DARKNESS

You hear my step
Come close, and stop.
I shut the door.
By the two-deck bed
And its breathing sheets
Houselight is killed
From off my breast.
I am unseen,
But sensed, but known,
And now begin

To be what I
Can never be,
But what I am
Within your dream:
A god or beast
Come true at last.
To one, I have
Like leaves grown here,
And furl my wings
As poplars sigh,

And slowly let
On him a breath
Drawn in a cloud,
In which he sees
Angelic hosts
Like blowing trees
Send me to earth
To root among
The secret soil
Of his dark room.

The other hears
A creature shed
Throughout the maze
The same long breath
As he conceives
That he no more
Desires to live
In blazing sun,
Nor shake to death
The animal

Of his own head.
I know what lies
Behind all words,
Like a beast, mismade,
Which finds its brain
Can sing alone
Without a sound
At what he is
And cannot change,
Or like a god

Which slowly breathes
Eternal life
Upon a soul
In deepest sleep.
My heart's one move
Comes now, and now.
A god strikes root
On touching earth.
A beast can hold
The thought of self

Between his horns
Until it shines.
That you may feel
What I must be
And cannot know
By standing here,
My sons, I bring
These beings home
Into your room.
They are. I am.

A SCREENED PORCH IN THE COUNTRY

All of them are sitting
Inside a lamp of coarse wire
And being in all directions
Shed upon darkness,
Their bodies softening to shadow, until
They come to rest out in the yard
In a kind of blurred golden country
In which they more deeply lie
Than if they were being created
Of Heavenly light.

Where they are floating beyond
Themselves, in peace,
Where they have laid down
Their souls and not known it,
The smallest creatures,
As every night they do,
Come to the edge of them
And sing, if they can,
Or, if they can't, simply shine
Their eyes back, sitting on haunches,

Pulsating and thinking of music.
Occasionally, something weightless
Touches the screen
With its body, dies,
Or is unmurmuringly hurt,
But mainly nothing happens
Except that a family continues
To be laid down
In the midst of its nightly creatures,
Not one of which openly comes

Into the golden shadow
Where the people are lying,
Emitted by their own house
So humanly that they become
More than human, and enter the place
Of small, blindly singing things,
Seeming to rejoice
Perpetually,without effort,
Without knowing why
Or how they do it.

THE DREAM FLOOD

I ask and receive
The secret of falling unharmed
Forty nights from the darkness of Heaven,
Coming down in sheets and in atoms
Until I descend to the moon

Where it lies on the ground
And finds in my surface the shining
It knew it must have in the end.
No longer increasing, I stand
Taking sunlight transmitted by stone,

And then begin over fields
To expand like a mind seeking truth,
Piling fathoms of brightness in valleys,
Letting no hilltop break through me.
As I rise, the moon rises also

As the reborn look of creation
In the animals' eyes,
In the eyes of horses in stables
Who feel their warm heaviness swarm
Out of their mouths like their souls;

Their bodies in cell blocks of wood
Hang like a dust that has taken
Their shapes without knowing of horses.
When the straight sun strikes them at last
Their grains congeal as they must

And nail their scuffed hoofs to the earth.
I withdraw, in feeling the cloud

Of Heaven call dazzlingly to me
To drop off my horses and forests,
To leave a vague mist in the valleys

And the hilltops steaming.
O grasses and fence wire of glory
That have burned like a coral with depth,
Understand that I have stood shining
About loved and abandoned women:

For acres around their thin beds
Which lifted like mesmerized tables
And danced in mid-air of their rooms
Like the chairs that blind children dance with,
So that each, hanging deep in her morning

Rose-colored bath, shall implore
Those impotent waters, and sunlight
Straining in vain
With her lost, dead weight:
"Lift. I am dreaming. Lift."

THE SCRATCH

Once hid in a fiery twist
Of brier, it binds my wrist.
In this marked place, on a stone,
I watchfully sit down
To lift it wisely, and see
Blood come, as at a play,
Which shall fall outside my life.
It knows neither stone nor leaf,
Nor how it has come from my heart
To find its true color in light.
The glaze of my death is upon it
In the shadowy sun, and yet
A merciful rust shall set in
To kill, not me, but my pain.
My arm opened up by a thorn,
I feel the no-soul of the rock;
I hear, through the trees, the cock
Shout out his long-necked cry.
My patience comes over the wood,
And, caught in the silence of blood,
The wind in the leaves stands still
And delivers its green to my will.
I raise my other-armed sleeve,
And wipe, in a kind of love,
The wellspring of love from its bed,
And, glancing about for the dead,
Look distantly off at my blood
As it forms upon air, as if
It were the first blood of my life,
And the last thing of earth that I owned.
I conjure up sons, all crowned,
Who this drop shall not inherit,

And women who shall not share it,
Who might have borne me that son
To sit on a moss-backed stone
And master the kingdom of silence
Forever: as I do, once.
I feel more alive thereby
Than when the same blood in my eye
Of sleep, brought my real son,
Or my wife, that heavenly one.
I have had no vision but this
Of blood unable to pass
Between father and son,
Yet wedding the brain and the stone,
The cock's cutting cry and the thorn,
And binding me, whole, in a wood,
To a prince of impossible blood.
The rock shall inherit my soul.
The gem at my wrist is dull,
And may or may never fall.
Which will be, I do not know.
I shall dream of a crown till I do.

HUNTING CIVIL WAR RELICS AT
NIMBLEWILL CREEK

As he moves the mine detector
A few inches over the ground,
Making it vitally float
Among the ferns and weeds,
I come into this war
Slowly, with my one brother,
Watching his face grow deep
Between the earphones,
For I can tell
If we enter the buried battle
Of Nimblewill
Only by his expression.

Softly he wanders, parting
The grass with a dreaming hand.
No dead cry yet takes root
In his clapped ears
Or can be seen in his smile.
But underfoot I feel
The dead regroup,
The burst metals all in place,
The battle lines be drawn
Anew to include us
In Nimblewill,
And I carry the shovel and pick

More as if they were
Bright weapons that I bore.
A bird's cry breaks
In two, and into three parts.
We cross the creek; the cry

Shifts into another,
Nearer, bird, and is
Like the shout of a shadow—
Lived-with, appallingly close—
Or the soul, pronouncing
"Nimblewill":
Three tones; your being changes.

We climb the bank;
A faint light glows
On my brother's mouth.
I listen, as two birds fight
For a single voice, but he
Must be hearing the grave,
In pieces, all singing
To his clamped head,
For he smiles as if
He rose from the dead within
Green Nimblewill
And stood in his grandson's shape.

No shot from the buried war
Shall kill me now,
For the dead have waited here
A hundred years to create
Only the look on the face
Of my one brother,
Who stands among them, offering
A metal dish
Afloat in the trembling weeds,
With a long-buried light on his lips

At Nimblewill
And the dead outsinging two birds.

I choke the handle
Of the pick, and fall to my knees
To dig wherever he points,
To bring up mess tin or bullet,
To go underground
Still singing, myself,
Without a sound,
Like a man who renounces war,
Or one who shall lift up the past,
Not breathing "Father,"
At Nimblewill,
But saying, "Fathers! Fathers!"

THE TWIN FALLS

They fall through my life and surround me
Where I stand on a stone held between them,
And help them sing down the lifting

Of leaves in the springtime valley.
If I move my bare arms, the wings
Of water shake and are whiter.

I dance on the unshaken stone
And the rock rises up in my voice
As water the shape of my shoulders

Falls past without passing or moving.
Lifting up the blind spirit of bedrock,
My voice falls in waves on the green

Held up in a storm to receive it,
Where trees with their roots in my standing
Are singing it back to surround me

And telling me how my light body
Falls through the still years of my life
On great, other wings than its own.

THE HOSPITAL WINDOW

I have just come down from my father.
Higher and higher he lies
Above me in a blue light
Shed by a tinted window.
I drop through six white floors
And then step out onto pavement.

Still feeling my father ascend,
I start to cross the firm street,
My shoulder blades shining with all
The glass the huge building can raise.
Now I must turn round and face it,
And know his one pane from the others.

Each window possesses the sun
As though it burned there on a wick.
I wave, like a man catching fire.
All the deep-dyed windowpanes flash,
And, behind them, all the white rooms
They turn to the color of Heaven.

Ceremoniously, gravely, and weakly,
Dozens of pale hands are waving
Back, from inside their flames.
Yet one pure pane among these
Is the bright, erased blankness of nothing.
I know that my father is there,

In the shape of his death still living.
The traffic increases around me
Like a madness called down on my head.
The horns blast at me like shotguns,

And drivers lean out, driven crazy—
But now my propped-up father

Lifts his arm out of stillness at last.
The light from the window strikes me
And I turn as blue as a soul,
As the moment when I was born.
I am not afraid for my father—
Look! He is grinning; he is not

Afraid for my life, either,
As the wild engines stand at my knees
Shredding their gears and roaring,
And I hold each car in its place
For miles, inciting its horn
To blow down the walls of the world

That the dying may float without fear
In the bold blue gaze of my father.
Slowly I move to the sidewalk
With my pin-tingling hand half dead
At the end of my bloodless arm.
I carry it off in amazement,

High, still higher, still waving,
My recognized face fully mortal,
Yet not; not at all, in the pale,
Drained, otherworldly, stricken,
Created hue of stained glass.
I have just come down from my father.

PART FOUR

THE MAGUS

It is time for the others to come.
This child is no more than a god.

No cars are moving this night.
The lights in the houses go out.

I put these out with the rest.
From his crib, the child begins

To shine, letting forth one ray
Through the twelve simple bars of his bed

Down into the trees, where two
Long-lost other men shall be drawn

Slowly up to the brink of the house,
Slowly in through the breath on the window.

But how did I get in this room?
Is this my son, or another's?

75

Where is the woman to tell me
How my face is lit up by his body?

It is time for the others to come.
An event more miraculous yet

Is the thing I am shining to tell you.
This child is no more than a child.

ANTIPOLIS

Through the town-making stones I step lightly.
Each thing in the market place looks
Clear through me, not able to help it.
Squid lounging in death in their barrel
See me staring through life down among them.
They deepen the depth of their gaze.
The eyes of the dead hold me brightly.
I take all their looks into mine
And lift them up

Alive, and carry them out through the door
The Greeks made to give on the sea.
The world opens wide and turns blue.
My heart shines in me like sunlight.
I scramble up sill after sill,
Past windows where women are washing
My strange, heavy, foreigner's clothes.
My voice in amazement dwindles
To that of a child,

And with it I call to my son,
Who reads Greek somewhere below me.
He answers; a dead tongue sings.
I leap to the bread-colored rampart,
And stroll there, sweating and staring
Down into the powder-blue ocean
With dozens of dead, round, all-seeing eyes
In my head, which have seen ships sink
Through this water

And gods rise, wearing their sails.
A hundred feet over the ocean,

My hands dead white with the flour
Of the market, knowing and saying
The same timeless thought as the sun,
Which thinks of itself in its glory
As Pericles' head on a coin,
I hear in my voice two children,
My son and my soul,

Sing to each other through ages.
In the windows, men with their women
Among my dark garments burn cleanly.
Because I am drunk on the rampart,
My son reads Homer more deeply,
And the blue sea has caught me alive
In my own glance, the look of some daring,
Unbelieved, believing and dancing
Most loving creature.

THE CHANGE

Blue, unstirrable, dreaming.
The hammerhead goes by the boat,
Passing me slowly in looking.

He has singled me out from the others;
He has put his blue gaze in my brain.
The strength of creation sees through me:

The world is yet blind as beginning.
The shark's brutal form never changes.
No millions of years shall yet turn him

From himself to a man in love,
Yet I feel that impossible man
Hover near, emerging from darkness,

Like a creature of light from the ocean.
He is what I would make of myself
In ten million years, if I could,

And arise from my brute of a body
To a thing the world never thought of
In a place as apparent as Heaven.

I name the blue shark in the water,
And the heart of my brain has spoken
To me, like an unknown brother,

Gently of ends and beginnings,
Gently of sources and outcomes,
Impossible, brighter than sunlight.

AUTUMN

I see the tree think it will turn
Brown, and tomorrow at dawn
It will change as it thinks it will change,

But faster, bringing in orange,
And smoking and king-killing gold.
The fire of death shall change colors,

But before its rich images die,
Some green will be thought of in glory.
The dead shall withhold it until

The sleep of the world take on
The air of awaiting an angel
To descend into Hell, and to blow

With his once-a-year breath upon grass roots,
And deliver the year from its thinking
To the mindless one color of life.

SNOW ON A SOUTHERN STATE

Alongside the train I labor
To change wholly into my spirit,
As the place of my birth falls upward

Into the snow,
And my pale, sealed face looks in
From the world where it ripples and sails,
Sliding through culverts,

Plunging through tunnels while flakes
Await my long, streaming return
As they wait for this country to rise

And become something else in mid-air.
With a just-opened clicking, I come
Forth into fresh, buried meadows
Of muffled night light

Where people still sit on their porches
Screened in for eternal summer,
Watching the snow

Like grated shadow sift
Impossibly to them.
Through the window I tell them dumbly
That the snow is like

A man, stretched out upon landscape
And a spotless berth,
Who is only passing through

Their country, who means no harm:
Who stares in distrust at his ghost
Also flying, feet first, through the distance.
Numbly, the lips of his spirit

Move, and a fur-bearing steeple looms up
Through the heart of his mirrored breast.
The small town where he was born

Assembles around it,
The neon trying, but obviously unreal,
The parked cars clumsily letting
Pureness, a blinding burden,

Come slowly upon them.
All are still, all are still,
For the breath-holding window and I

Only must move through the silence,
Bearing my huge, prone ghost
Up, out, and now flying over
The vapor-lamp-glowing high school

Into the coming fields
Like a thing we cannot put down.
Yet the glass gives out of my image

And the laid clicking dies, as the land
All around me shines with the power
Of renewing my youth
By changing the place where I lived it.

There is nothing here, now, to watch
The bedclothes whirl into flakes.
What should be warm in these blankets

Has powdered down into its own
Steel-blue and feathery visions
Of weddings opposed by the world:
Is hovering over

A dead cotton field, which awaits
Its touch as awaiting completion:
Is building the pinewoods again

For this one night of their lives:
With the equilibrium
Of bones, is falling, falling,
Falling into the river.

TO LANDRUM GUY, BEGINNING TO WRITE AT SIXTY

One man in a house
Consumed by the effort of listening,
Sets down a worried phrase upon a paper.
It is poor, though it has come

From the table as out of a wall,
From his hand as out of his heart.

To sixty years it has come
At the same rate of time as he.
He cannot tell it, ever, what he thinks.
It is time, he says, he must

Be thinking of nothing but singing,
Be singing of nothing but love.

But the right word cannot arrive
Through the dark, light house of one man
With his savage hand on a book,
With a cricket seizing slowly on his ear:

One man in a house cannot hear
His ear, with his hair falling out from the quick.

Even to himself he cannot say
Except with not one word,
How he hears there is no more light
Than this, nor any word

More anywhere: how he is drunk
On hope, and why he calls himself mad.

Weeping is steadily built, and does not fall
From the shadow sitting slowly behind him
On the wall, like an angel who writes him a letter
To tell him his only talent is too late

To tell, to weep, to speak, or to begin
Here, or ever. Here, where he begins.

FACING AFRICA

These are stone jetties,
And, in the close part of the night,
Connected to my feet by long
Warm, dangling shadows
On the buttressed water,
Boats are at rest.

Beyond, the harbor mouth opens
Much as you might believe
A human mouth would open
To say that all things are a darkness.
I sit believing this
As the boats beneath me dissolve

And shake with a haunted effort
To come into being again,
And my son nods at my side,
Looking out also
Into dark, through the painted
Living shadows of dead-still hulls

Toward where we imagine Africa
To bloom late at night
Like a lamp of sand held up,
A top-heavy hourglass, perhaps,
With its heaped, eternal grains
Falling, falling

Into the lower, green part
Which gives off quick, leafy flashes
Like glimpses of lightning.
We strain to encounter that image

Halfway from its shore to ours:
To understand

The undermined glowing of sand
Lifted at midnight
Somewhere far out above water,
The effortless flicker of trees
Where a rumor of beasts moves slowly
Like wave upon wave.

What life have we entered by this?
Here, where our bodies are,
With a green and gold light on his face,
My staring child's hand is in mine,
And in the stone
Fear like a dancing of peoples.

INSIDE THE RIVER

Dark, deeply. A red.
All levels moving
A given surface.
Break this. Step down.
Follow your right
Foot nakedly in
To another body.
Put on the river
Like a fleeing coat,
A garment of motion,
Tremendous, immortal.
Find a still root

To hold you in it.
Let flowing create
A new, inner being:
As the source in the mountain
Gives water in pulses,
These can be felt at
The heart of the current.
And here it is only
One wandering step
Forth, to the sea.
Your freed hair floating
Out of your brain,

Wait for a coming
And swimming idea.
Live like the dead
In their flying feeling.
Loom as a ghost
When life pours through it.

Crouch in the secret
Released underground
With the earth of the fields
All around you, gone
Into purposeful grains
That stream like dust

In a holy hallway.
Weight more changed
Than that of one
Now being born,
Let go the root.
Move with the world
As the deep dead move,
Opposed to nothing.
Release. Enter the sea
Like a winding wind.
No. Rise. Draw breath.
Sing. See no one.

THE SALT MARSH

Once you have let the first blade
Spring back behind you
To the way it has always been,
You no longer know where you are.
All you can see are the tall
Stalks of sawgrass, not sawing,
But each of them holding its tip
Exactly at the level where your hair

Begins to grow from your forehead.
Wherever you come to is
The same as before,
With the same blades of oversized grass,
And wherever you stop, the one
Blade just in front of you leans,
That one only, and touches you
At the place where your hair begins

To grow; at that predestined touch
Your spine tingles crystally, like salt,
And the image of a crane occurs,
Each flap of its wings creating
Its feathers anew, this time whiter,
As the sun destroys all points
Of the compass, refusing to move
From its chosen noon.

Where is the place you have come from
With your buried steps full of new roots?
You cannot leap up to look out,
Yet you do not sink,
But seem to grow, and the sound,

The oldest of sounds, is your breath
Sighing like acres.
If you stand as you are for long,

Green panic may finally give
Way to another sensation,
For when the embodying wind
Rises, the grasses begin to weave
A little, then all together,
Not bending enough for you
To see your way clear of the swaying,
But moving just the same,

And nothing prevents your bending
With them, helping their wave
Upon wave upon wave upon wave
By not opposing,
By willing your supple inclusion
Among fields without promise of harvest,
In their marvelous, spiritual walking
Everywhere, anywhere.

IN THE MOUNTAIN TENT

I am hearing the shape of the rain
Take the shape of the tent and believe it,
Laying down all around where I lie
A profound, unspeakable law.
I obey, and am free-falling slowly

Through the thought-out leaves of the wood
Into the minds of animals.
I am there in the shining of water
Like dark, like light, out of Heaven.

I am there like the dead, or the beast
Itself, which thinks of a poem—
Green, plausible, living, and holy—
And cannot speak, but hears,
Called forth from the waiting of things,

A vast, proper, reinforced crying
With the sifted, harmonious pause,
The sustained intake of all breath
Before the first word of the Bible.

At midnight water dawns
Upon the held skulls of the foxes
And weasels and tousled hares
On the eastern side of the mountain.
Their light is the image I make

As I wait as if recently killed,
Receptive, fragile, half-smiling,
My brow watermarked with the mark
On the wing of a moth

And the tent taking shape on my body
Like ill-fitting, Heavenly clothes.
From holes in the ground comes my voice
In the God-silenced tongue of the beasts.
"I shall rise from the dead," I am saying.

tent it almost conforming to human shape

Downward & upward motions -

Resurrection - eventually rises again

Water

HELMETS

PART ONE

THE DUSK OF HORSES

Right under their noses, the green
Of the field is paling away
Because of something fallen from the sky.

They see this, and put down
Their long heads deeper in grass
That only just escapes reflecting them

As the dream of a millpond would.
The color green flees over the grass
Like an insect, following the red sun over

The next hill. The grass is white.
There is no cloud so dark and white at once;
There is no pool at dawn that deepens

Their faces and thirsts as this does.
Now they are feeding on solid
Cloud, and, one by one,

With nails as silent as stars among the wood
Hewed down years ago and now rotten,
The stalls are put up around them.

Now if they lean, they come
On wood on any side. Not touching it, they sleep.
No beast ever lived who understood

What happened among the sun's fields,
Or cared why the color of grass
Fled over the hill while he stumbled,

Led by the halter to sleep
On his four taxed, worthy legs.
Each thinks he awakens where

The sun is black on the rooftop,
That the green is dancing in the next pasture,
And that the way to sleep

In a cloud, or in a risen lake,
Is to walk as though he were still
In the drained field standing, head down,

To pretend to sleep when led,
And thus to go under the ancient white
Of the meadow, as green goes

And whiteness comes up through his face
Holding stars and rotten rafters,
Quiet, fragrant, and relieved.

FENCE WIRE

Too tight, it is running over
Too much of this ground to be still
Or to do anything but tremble
And disappear left and right
As far as the eye can see

Over hills, through woods,
Down roads, to arrive at last
Again where it connects,
Coming back from the other side
Of animals, defining their earthly estate

As the grass becomes snow
While they are standing and dreaming
Of grass and snow.
The winter hawk that sits upon its post,
Feeling the airy current of the wires,

Turns into a robin, sees that this is wrong,
Then into a boy, and into a man who holds
His palm on the top tense strand
With the whole farm feeding slowly
And nervously into his hand.

If the wire were cut anywhere
All his blood would fall to the ground
And leave him standing and staring
With a face as white as a Hereford's.
From years of surrounding grain,

Cows, horses, machinery trying to turn
To rust, the humming arrives each second,
A sound that arranges these acres
And holds them highstrung and enthralled.
Because of the light, chilled hand

On the top thread tuned to an E
Like the low string of a guitar,
The dead corn is more
Balanced in death than it was,
The animals more aware

Within the huge human embrace
Held up and borne out of sight
Upon short, unbreakable poles
Wherethrough the ruled land intones
Like a psalm: properly,

With its eyes closed,
Whether on the side of the animals
Or not, whether disappearing
Right, left, through trees or down roads,
Whether outside, around, or in.

AT DARIEN BRIDGE

The sea here used to look
As if many convicts had built it,

Standing deep in their ankle chains,
Ankle-deep in the water, to smite

The land and break it down to salt.
I was in this bog as a child

When they were all working all day
To drive the pilings down.

I thought I saw the still sun
Strike the side of a hammer in flight

And from it a sea bird be born
To take off over the marshes.

As the gray climbs the side of my head
And cuts my brain off from the world,

I walk and wish mainly for birds,
For the one bird no one has looked for

To spring again from a flash
Of metal, perhaps from the scratched

Wedding band on my ring finger.
Recalling the chains of their feet,

I stand and look out over grasses
At the bridge they built, long abandoned,

Breaking down into water at last,
And long, like them, for freedom

Or death, or to believe again
That they worked on the ocean to give it

The unchanging, hopeless look
Out of which all miracles leap.

CHENILLE

There are two facing peacocks
    Or a ship flapping
On its own white tufted sail
At roadside, near a mill;

Flamingoes also are hanging
    By their bills on bedspreads
And an occasional mallard.
These you can buy anywhere.
They are made by machine
From a sanctioned, unholy pattern
Rigid with industry.
They hoard the smell of oil

And hum like looms all night
    Into your pores, reweaving
Your body from bobbins.
There is only one quiet

Place — in a scuppernong arbor —
    Where animals as they
Would be, are born into sleep-cloth:
A middle-aged man's grandmother
Sits in the summer green light
Of leaves, gone toothless
For eating grapes better,
And pulls the animals through

With a darning needle:
    Deer, rabbits and birds,
Red whales and unicorns,
Winged elephants, crowned ants:

Beasts that cannot be thought of
        By the wholly sane
Rise up in the rough, blurred
Flowers of fuzzy cloth
In only their timeless outlines
Like the beasts of Heaven:
Those sketched out badly, divinely
By stars not wholly sane.

Love, I have slept in that house.
        There it was winter.
The tattered moonfields crept
Through the trellis, and fell

In vine-tangled shade on my face
        Like thrown-away knitting
Before cloud came and dimmed
Those scars from off me.
My fingernails chilled
To the bone. I called
For another body to be
With me, and warm us both.

A unicorn neighed; I folded
        His neck in my arms
And was safe, as he lay down.
All night, from thickening Heaven,

Someone up there kept throwing
        Bedspreads upon me.
Softly I called, and they came:
The ox and the basilisk,

The griffin, the phoenix, the lion —
Light-bodied, only the essence,
The tufted, creative starfields
Behind the assembling clouds —

The snake from the apple tree came
    To save me from freezing,
And at last the lung-winged ship
On its own sail scented with potash

Fell sighing upon us all.
    The last two nails
Of cold died out in my nostrils
Under the dance-weight of beasts.
I lay, breathing like thread,
An inspired outline of myself,
As rain began greatly to fall,
And closed the door of the Ark.

ON THE COOSAWATTEE

1. By Canoe Through the Fir Forest

Into the slain tons of needles,
On something like time and dark knowledge
That cannot be told, we are riding
Over white stones forward through fir trees,
To follow whatever the river
Through the clasping of roots follows deeply.

As we go inward, more trunks
Climb from the edge of the water
And turn on the banks and stand growing.
The nerves in the patches of tree-light
On the ripples can feel no death,
But shake like the wings of angels

With light hard-pressed to keep up
Though it is in place on each feather.
Heavy woods in one movement around us
Flow back along either side
Bringing in more essential curves;
Small stones in their thousands turn corners

Under water and bear us on
Through the glittering, surfacing wingbeats
Cast from above. As we pass over,
As we pass through each hover of gold,
We lift up our blades from the water
And the blades of our shoulders,

Our rowing-muscles, our wings,
Are still and tremble, undying,

Drifting deeper into the forest.
Each light comes into our life
Past the man in front's changed hair
Then along the wing-balancing floor

And then onto me and one eye
And into my mouth for an instant.
The stones beneath us grow rounder
As I taste the fretted light fall
Through living needles to be here
Like a word I can feed on forever

Or believe like a vision I have
Or want to conceive out of greenness.
While the world fades, it is *becoming*.
As the trees shut away all seeing,
In my mouth I mix it with sunlight.
Here, in the dark, it is *being*.

II. *Below Ellijay*

Coming into Ellijay on the green
Idling freeway of the broad river
From the hill farms and pine woods,
We saw first the little stores
That backed down the red clay banks,
The blue flash of bottleglass
And the rippled tin heat haze of sheds

Where country mechanics were frying.
A poultry-processing plant
Smoked in the late morning air;

The bridge we rode under clattered
As we wound back out into fields.
But the water that held us had changed;
The town had slowed it and used it;

The wind had died in the tool sheds.
When we looked overboard, we knew.
Each thing was mistakenly feathered,
Muffled thickly in cast-off whiteness:
Each log was bedraggled in plumage
And accepting more feathers from water;
Each boulder under the green

Was becoming a lewd, setting hen
Moultingly under us brooding
In the sick, buried wind of the river,
Wavering, dying, increasing
From the plucked refuse of the plant,
And beside us uselessly floated —
Following, dipping, returning,

Turning frankly around to eye us,
To eye something else, to eye
Us again — a skinned chicken head,
Its gaze unperturbed and abiding.
All morning we floated on feathers
Among the drawn heads which appeared
Everywhere, from under the logs

Of feathers, from upstream behind us,
Lounging back to us from ahead,
Until we believed ourselves doomed
And the planet corrupted forever,

With stones turned to pullets, not struggling
But into more monstrousness shed,
Our canoe trailing more and more feathers

And the eye of the devil upon us
Closing drunkenly in from all sides,
And could have been on the Styx
In the blaze of noon, till we felt
The quickening pulse of the rapids
And entered upon it like men
Who sense that the world can be cleansed

Among rocks pallid only with water,
And plunged there like the unborn
Who see earthly streams without taint
Flow beneath them, while their wing feathers
Slough off behind them in Heaven
As they dress in the blinding clothes
Of nakedness for their fall.

III. *The Inundation*

Down there is a stone that holds my deepest sleep
And buries it deeper and deeper
Under the green, skinny lake
That is going back into the Georgia hills
And climbing them day and night
Behind the new dam.

And there is another stone, that boiled with white,
Where Braselton and I clung and fought
With our own canoe

That flung us in the rapids we had ridden
So that it might turn and take on
A ton of mountain water

And swing and bear down through the flying cloud
Of foam upon our violent rock
And pin us there.
With our backs to the wall of that boulder,
We yelled and kept it off us as we could,
Broke both paddles,

Then wedged it with the paddle stumps up over
The rock till the hull split, and it leapt and fell
Into the afterfall.
In life preservers we whirled ourselves away
And floated aimlessly down into calm water,
Turning like objects,

Then crawled upon shore and were found in the afternoon
By Lucas Gentry and his hunting dog, asleep
On a vast, gentle stone.
At a touch we woke, and followed the strange woods boy
Up the bluff, looking down on the roaring river's
Last day in its bed.

And now I cannot sleep at all, until I think
Of the Coosa, out of a clear blue sky
Overswelling its banks,
Its great stones falling through it into dark,
Its creeks becoming inlets, where water
Skiers already poise.

Over me it rises, too, but breathable, like cloud,
A green and silver cloud above which quiet
Lucas Gentry stands.
His dog whines, as the last rock of the wild river
Goes under, its white water lapses green,
And the leaping stone

Where we almost died takes on the settled repose
Of that other where we lay down and met
Our profoundest sleep
Rising from it to us, as the battered sides
Of the canoe gave deeper and deeper shade,
And Lucas Gentry,

Who may have been the accepting spirit of the place
Come to call us to higher ground,
Bent to raise
Us from the sleep of the yet-to-be-drowned,
There, with the black dream of the dead canoe
Over our faces.

WINTER TROUT

In the concrete cells of the hatchery
He nourished a dream of living
Under the ice, the long preparations
For the strange heat of feeling slowly

Roofs melt to a rhythmic green,
But now, in the first cold of freedom,
Riding motionless under the road
Of ice, shaping the heart

Of the buried stream with his tail,
He knows that his powers come
From the fire and stillness of freezing.
With the small tremors of his form

The banks shift imperceptibly,
Shift back, tremble, settle,
Shift, all within utter stillness.
I keep in my quiver now

An arrow whose head is half-missing.
It is useless, but I will not change
The pulled, broken tooth of its head
For I have walked upon banks

Shaken with the watchfulness of trout
Like walking barefoot in sleep
On the swaying tips of a grainfield,
On the long, just-bending stems,

Almost weightless, able to leap
Great distances, yet not leaping
Because each step on that ground
Gave a new sense of limitless hope.

Under the ice the trout rode,
Trembling, in the mastered heart
Of the creek, with what he could do.
I set myself up as a statue

With a bow, my red woolen back
Climbed slowly by thoughtful brambles
And dead beggar-lice, to shoot
At an angle down through the shadow

Of ice, and spear the trout
With a shot like Ulysses'
Through the ax heads, with the great weapon.
I shot, and the trout did not move

But was gone, and the banks
Went rigid under my feet
As the arrow floated away
Under the paving of ice.

I froze my right hand to retrieve it
As a blessing or warning,
As a sign of the penalties
For breaking into closed worlds

Where the wary controllers lie
At the heart of their power,
A pure void of shadowy purpose
Where the gods live, attuning the world,

Laying plans for the first green
They ever have lived, to melt
The ice from their great crowns.
Their secret enemies break

Like statues, as the king rises slowly,
Keeping only the thinnest film
Of his element — imagination —
Before his eyes as he lifts

Into spring, with the wood upside down
Balanced perfectly in all its leaves
And roots as he deeply has
All winter made provision for,

The surface full of gold flakes
Of the raw undersides of leaves,
And the thing seen right,
For once, that winter bought.

SPRINGER MOUNTAIN

Four sweaters are woven upon me,
All black, all sweating and waiting,
And a sheepherder's coat's wool hood,
Buttoned strainingly, holds my eyes
With their sight deepfrozen outside them
From their gaze toward a single tree.
I am here where I never have been,
In the limbs of my warmest clothes,
Waiting for light to crawl, weakly
From leaf to dead leaf onto leaf
Down the western side of the mountain.
Deer sleeping in light far above me

Have already woken, and moved,
In step with the sun moving strangely
Down toward the dark knit of my thicket
Where my breath takes shape on the air
Like a white helmet come from the lungs.
The one tree I hope for goes inward
And reaches the limbs of its gold.
My eyesight hangs partly between
Two twigs on the upslanting ground,
Then steps like a god from the dead
Wet of a half-rotted oak log
Steeply into the full of my brow.
My thighbones groaningly break

Upward, releasing my body
To climb, and to find among humus
New insteps made of snapped sticks.
On my back the faggot of arrows
Rattles and scratches its feathers.

I go up over logs slowly
On my painfully reborn legs,
My ears putting out vast hearing
Among the invisible animals,

Passing under thin branches held still,
Kept formed all night as they were
By the thought of predictable light.
The sun comes openly in
To my mouth, and is blown out white,

But no deer is anywhere near me.
I sit down and wait as in darkness.

The sweat goes dead at the roots

Of my hair: a deer is created
Descending, then standing and looking.
The sun stands and waits for his horns

To move. I may be there, also,
Between them, in head bones uplifted
Like a man in an animal tree
Nailed until light comes:
A dream of the unfeared hunter
Who has formed in his brain in the dark
And rose with light into his horns,
Naked, and I have turned younger

At forty than I ever have been.
I hang my longbow on a branch.

The buck leaps away and then stops,
And I step forward, stepping out

Of my shadow and pulling over
My head one dark heavy sweater
After another, my dungarees falling
Till they can be kicked away,
Boots, socks, all that is on me
Off. The world catches fire.
I put an unbearable light
Into breath skinned alive of its garments:
I think, beginning with laurel,
Like a beast loving
With the whole god bone of his horns:
The green of excess is upon me
Like deer in fir thickets in winter
Stamping and dreaming of men
Who will kneel with them naked to break
The ice from streams with their faces
And drink from the lifespring of beasts.
He is moving. I am with him

Down the shuddering hillside moving
Through trees and around, inside
And out of stumps and groves
Of laurel and slash pine,
Through hip-searing branches and thorn
Brakes, unprotected and sure,
Winding down to the waters of life

Where they stand petrified in a creek bed
Yet melt and flow from the hills
At the touch of an animal visage,

Rejoicing wherever I come to
With the gold of my breast unwrapped,
My crazed laughter pure as good church-cloth,
My brain dazed and pointed with trying
To grow horns, glad that it cannot,
For a few steps deep in the dance
Of what I most am and should be
And can be only once in this life.
He is gone below, and I limp
To look for my clothes in the world,

A middle-aged, softening man
Grinning and shaking his head
In amazement to last him forever.
I put on the warm-bodied wool,
The four sweaters inside out,
The bootlaces dangling and tripping,
Then pick my tense bow off the limb
And turn with the unwinding hooftracks,
In my good, tricked clothes,
To hunt, under Springer Mountain,
Deer for the first and last time.

PART TWO

CHERRYLOG ROAD

Off Highway 106
At Cherrylog Road I entered
The '34 Ford without wheels,
Smothered in kudzu,
With a seat pulled out to run
Corn whiskey down from the hills,

And then from the other side
Crept into an Essex
With a rumble seat of red leather
And then out again, aboard
A blue Chevrolet, releasing
The rust from its other color,

Reared up on three building blocks.
None had the same body heat;
I changed with them inward, toward
The weedy heart of the junkyard,
For I knew that Doris Holbrook
Would escape from her father at noon

And would come from the farm
To seek parts owned by the sun
Among the abandoned chassis,
Sitting in each in turn
As I did, leaning forward
As in a wild stock-car race

In the parking lot of the dead.
Time after time, I climbed in
And out the other side, like
An envoy or movie star
Met at the station by crickets.
A radiator cap raised its head,

Become a real toad or a kingsnake
As I neared the hub of the yard,
Passing through many states,
Many lives, to reach
Some grandmother's long Pierce-Arrow
Sending platters of blindness forth

From its nickel hubcaps
And spilling its tender upholstery
On sleepy roaches,
The glass panel in between
Lady and colored driver
Not all the way broken out,

The back-seat phone
Still on its hook.
I got in as though to exclaim,
"Let us go to the orphan asylum,

John; I have some old toys
For children who say their prayers."

I popped with sweat as I thought
I heard Doris Holbrook scrape
Like a mouse in the southern-state sun
That was eating the paint in blisters
From a hundred car tops and hoods.
She was tapping like code,

Loosening the screws,
Carrying off headlights,
Sparkplugs, bumpers,
Cracked mirrors and gear-knobs,
Getting ready, already,
To go back with something to show

Other than her lips' new trembling
I would hold to me soon, soon,
Where I sat in the ripped back seat
Talking over the interphone,
Praying for Doris Holbrook
To come from her father's farm

And to get back there
With no trace of me on her face
To be seen by her red-haired father
Who would change, in the squalling barn,
Her back's pale skin with a strop,
Then lay for me

In a bootlegger's roasting car
With a string-triggered 12-gauge shotgun
To blast the breath from the air.
Not cut by the jagged windshields,
Through the acres of wrecks she came
With a wrench in her hand,

Through dust where the blacksnake dies
Of boredom, and the beetle knows
The compost has no more life.
Someone outside would have seen
The oldest car's door inexplicably
Close from within:

I held her and held her and held her,
Convoyed at terrific speed
By the stalled, dreaming traffic around us,
So the blacksnake, stiff
With inaction, curved back
Into life, and hunted the mouse

With deadly overexcitement,
The beetles reclaimed their field
As we clung, glued together,
With the hooks of the seat springs
Working through to catch us red-handed
Amidst the gray, breathless batting

That burst from the seat at our backs.
We left by separate doors
Into the changed, other bodies
Of cars, she down Cherrylog Road

And I to my motorcycle
Parked like the soul of the junkyard

Restored, a bicycle fleshed
With power, and tore off
Up Highway 106, continually
Drunk on the wind in my mouth,
Wringing the handlebar for speed,
Wild to be wreckage forever.

THE SCARRED GIRL

All glass may yet be whole
She thinks, it may be put together
From the deep inner flashing of her face.
One moment the windshield held

The countryside, the green
Level fields and the animals,
And these must be restored
To what they were when her brow

Broke into them for nothing, and began
Its sparkling under the gauze.
Though the still, small war for her beauty
Is stitched out of sight and lost,

It is not this field that she thinks of.
It is that her face, buried
And held up inside the slow scars,
Knows how the bright, fractured world

Burns and pulls and weeps
To come together again.
The green meadow lying in fragments
Under the splintered sunlight,

The cattle broken in pieces
By her useless, painful intrusion
Know that her visage contains
The process and hurt of their healing,

The hidden wounds that can
Restore anything, bringing the glass

Of the world together once more,
All as it was when she struck,

All except her. The shattered field
Where they dragged the telescoped car
Off to be pounded to scrap
Waits for her to get up,

For her calm, unimagined face
To emerge from the yards of its wrapping,
Red, raw, mixed-looking but entire,
A new face, an old life,

To confront the pale glass it has dreamed
Made whole and backed with wise silver,
Held in other hands brittle with dread,
A doctor's, a lip-biting nurse's,

Who do not see what she sees
Behind her odd face in the mirror:
The pastures of earth and of heaven
Restored and undamaged, the cattle

Risen out of their jagged graves
To walk in the seamless sunlight
And a newborn countenance
Put upon everything,

Her beauty gone, but to hover
Near for the rest of her life,
And good no nearer, but plainly
In sight, and the only way.

KUDZU

Japan invades. Far Eastern vines
Run from the clay banks they are

Supposed to keep from eroding,
Up telephone poles,
Which rear, half out of leafage,
As though they would shriek,
Like things smothered by their own
Green, mindless, unkillable ghosts.
In Georgia, the legend says
That you must close your windows

At night to keep it out of the house.
The glass is tinged with green, even so,

As the tendrils crawl over the fields.
The night the kudzu has
Your pasture, you sleep like the dead.
Silence has grown Oriental
And you cannot step upon ground:
Your leg plunges somewhere
It should not, it never should be,
Disappears, and waits to be struck

Anywhere between sole and kneecap:
For when the kudzu comes,

The snakes do, and weave themselves
Among its lengthening vines,
Their spade heads resting on leaves,
Growing also, in earthly power
And the huge circumstance of concealment.

One by one the cows stumble in,
Drooling a hot green froth,
And die, seeing the wood of their stalls

Strain to break into leaf.
In your closed house, with the vine

Tapping your window like lightning,
You remember what tactics to use.
In the wrong yellow fog-light of dawn
You herd them in, the hogs,
Head down in their hairy fat,
The meaty troops, to the pasture.
The leaves of the kudzu quake
With the serpents' fear, inside

The meadow ringed with men
Holding sticks, on the country roads.

The hogs disappear in the leaves.
The sound is intense, subhuman,
Nearly human with purposive rage.
There is no terror
Sound from the snakes.
No one can see the desperate, futile
Striking under the leaf heads.
Now and then, the flash of a long

Living vine, a cold belly,
Leaps up, torn apart, then falls

127

Under the tussling surface.
You have won, and wait for frost,
When, at the merest touch
Of cold, the kudzu turns
Black, withers inward and dies,
Leaving a mass of brown strings
Like the wires of a gigantic switchboard.
You open your windows,

With the lightning restored to the sky
And no leaves rising to bury

You alive inside your frail house,
And you think, in the opened cold,
Of the surface of things and its terrors,
And of the mistaken, mortal
Arrogance of the snakes
As the vines, growing insanely, sent
Great powers into their bodies
And the freedom to strike without warning:

From them, though they killed
Your cattle, such energy also flowed

To you from the knee-high meadow
(It was as though you had
A green sword twined among
The veins of your growing right arm —
Such strength as you would not believe
If you stood alone in a proper
Shaved field among your safe cows—):
Came in through your closed

128

Leafy windows and almighty sleep
And prospered, till rooted out.

THE BEHOLDERS

Far away under us, they are mowing on the green steps
Of the valley, taking long, unending swings
Among the ripe wheat.
It is something about them growing,
Growing smaller, that makes us look up and see
That what has come over them is a storm.

It is a blue-black storm the shape of this valley,
And includes, perhaps, in its darkness,
Three men in the air
Taking long, limber swings, cutting water.
Swaths start to fall and, on earth,
The men come closer together as they mow.

Now in the last stand of wheat they bend.
From above, we watch over them like gods,
Our chins on our hands,
Our great eyes staring, our throats dry
And aching to cry down on their heads
Some curse or blessing,

Some word we have never known, but we feel
That when the right time arrives, and more stillness,
Lightning will leap
From our mouths in reasonless justice
As they arc their scythes more slowly, taking care
Not to look up.

As darkness increases there comes
A dancing into each of their swings,
A dancing like men in a cloud.
We two are coming together

Also, along the wall.
No lightning yet falls from us

Where their long hooks catch on the last of the sun
And the color of the wheat passes upward,
Drawn off like standing water
Into the cloud, turning green;
The field becomes whiter and darker,
And fire in us gathers and gathers

Not to call down death to touch brightly
The only metal for miles
In the hands of judged, innocent men,
But for our use only, who in the first sheaves of rain
Sit thunderstruck, having now the power to speak
With deadly intent of love.

THE POISONED MAN

When the rattlesnake bit, I lay
In a dream of the country, and dreamed
Day after day of the river,

Where I sat with a jackknife and quickly
Opened my sole to the water.
Blood shed for the sake of one's life

Takes on the hid shape of the channel,
Disappearing under logs and through boulders.
The freezing river poured on

And, as it took hold of my blood,
Leapt up round the rocks and boiled over.
I felt that my heart's blood could flow

Unendingly out of the mountain,
Splitting bedrock apart upon redness,
And the current of life at my instep

Give deathlessly as a spring.
Some leaves fell from trees and whirled under.
I saw my struck bloodstream assume,

Inside the cold path of the river,
The inmost routes of a serpent
Through grass, through branches and leaves.

When I rose, the live oaks were ashen
And the wild grass was dead without flame.
Through the blasted cornfield I hobbled,

My foot tied up in my shirt,
And met my old wife in the garden,
Where she reached for a withering apple.

I lay in the country and dreamed
Of the substance and course of the river
While the different colors of fever

Like quilt patches flickered upon me.
At last I arose, with the poison
Gone out of the seam of the scar,

And brought my wife eastward and weeping,
Through the copper fields springing alive
With the promise of harvest for no one.

IN THE MARBLE QUARRY

Beginning to dangle beneath
The wind that blows from the undermined wood,
   I feel the great pulley grind,

   The thread I cling to lengthen
And let me soaring and spinning down into marble,
   Hooked and weightlessly happy

   Where the squared sun shines
Back equally from all four sides, out of stone
   And years of dazzling labor,

   To land at last among men
Who cut with power saws a Parian whiteness
   And, chewing slow tobacco,

   Their eyebrows like frost,
Shunt house-sized blocks and lash them to cables
   And send them heavenward

   Into small-town banks,
Into the columns and statues of government buildings,
   But mostly graves.

   I mount my monument and rise
Slowly and spinningly from the white-gloved men
   Toward the hewn sky

   Out of the basement of light,
Sadly, lifted through time's blinding layers
   On perhaps my tombstone

In which the original shape
Michelangelo believed was in every rock upon earth
Is heavily stirring,

Surprised to be an angel,
To be waked in North Georgia by the ponderous play
Of men with ten-ton blocks

But no more surprised than I
To feel sadness fall off as though I myself
Were rising from stone

Held by a thread in midair,
Badly cut, local-looking, and totally uninspired,
Not a masterwork

Or even worth seeing at all
But the spirit of this place just the same,
Felt here as joy.

A FOLK SINGER OF THE THIRTIES

On a bed of gravel moving
Over the other gravel
Roadbed between the rails, I lay
As in my apartment now.
I felt the engine enter
A tunnel a half-mile away
And settled deeper
Into the stones of my sleep
Drifting through North Dakota.
I pulled them over me
For warmth, though it was summer,
And in the dark we pulled

Into the freight yards of Bismarck.
In the gravel car buried
To my nose in sledge-hammered stones,
My guitar beside me straining
Its breast beneath the rock,
I lay in the buzzing yards
And crimson hands swinging lights
Saw my closed eyes burn
Open and shine in their lanterns.
The yard bulls pulled me out,
Raining a rockslide of pebbles.
Bashed in the head, I lay

On the ground
As in my apartment now.
I spat out my teeth
Like corn, as they jerked me upright
To be an example for
The boys who would ride the freights

Looking for work, or for
Their American lives.
Four held me stretching against
The chalked red boards,
Spreading my hands and feet,
And nailed me to the boxcar
With twenty-penny nails.
I hung there open-mouthed
As though I had no more weight
Or voice. The train moved out.

Through the landscape I edged
And drifted, my head on my breast
As in my clean sheets now,
And went flying sideways through
The country, the rivers falling
Away beneath my safe
Immovable feet,
Close to me as they fell
Down under the boiling trestles,
And the fields and woods
Unfolded. Sometimes, behind me,
Going into the curves,
Cattle cried in unison,
Singing of stockyards
Where their tilted blood
Would be calmed and spilled.
I heard them until I sailed
Into the dark of the woods,
Flying always into the moonlight
And out again into rain
That filled my mouth

With a great life-giving word,
And into the many lights
The towns hung up for Christmas
Sales, the berries and tinsel,
And then out again
Into the countryside.
Everyone I passed

Could never believe what they saw,
But gave me one look
They would never forget, as I stood
In my overalls, stretched on the nails,
And went by, or stood
In the steaming night yards,
Waiting to couple on,
Overhanging the cattle coming
Into the cars from the night-lights.
The worst pain was when
We shuddered away from the platforms.
I lifted my head and croaked
Like a crow, and the nails
Vibrated with something like music
Endlessly clicking with movement
And the powerful, simple curves.
I learned where the oil lay
Under the fields,
Where the water ran
With the most industrial power,
Where the best corn would grow
And what manure to use
On any field that I saw.

If riches were there,
Whatever it was would light up
Like a bonfire seen through an eyelid
And begin to be words
That would go with the sound of the rails.
Ghostly bridges sprang up across rivers,
Mills towered where they would be,
Slums tottered, and buildings longed
To bear up their offices.
I hung for years
And in the end knew it all
Through pain: the land,
The future of profits and commerce
And also humility
Without which none of it mattered.
In the stockyards east of Chicago

One evening, the orphans assembled
Like choir boys
And drew the nails from my hands
And from my accustomed feet.
I stumbled with them to their homes
In Hooverville

And began to speak
In a chapel of galvanized tin
Of what one wishes for
When streaming alone into woods
And out into sunlight and moonlight
And when having a station lamp bulb
In one eye and not the other
And under the bites

Of snowflakes and clouds of flies
And the squandered dust of the prairies
That will not settle back
Beneath the crops.
In my head the farms
And industrial sites were burning
To produce.
One night, I addressed the A.A.,
Almost singing,
And in the fiery,
Unconsummated desire

For drink that rose around me
From those mild-mannered men,
I mentioned a place for a shoe store
That I had seen near the yards
As a blackened hulk with potential.
A man rose up,
Took a drink from a secret bottle,
And hurried out of the room.
A year later to the day
He knelt at my feet
In a silver suit of raw silk.
I sang to industrial groups
With a pearl-inlaid guitar

And plucked the breast-straining strings
With a nail that had stood through my hand.
I could not keep silent

About the powers of water,
Or where the coal beds lay quaking,

Or where electrical force
Should stalk in its roofless halls
Alone through the night wood,
Where the bridges should leap,
Striving with all their might
To connect with the other shore
To carry the salesmen.
I gave all I knew
To the owners, and they went to work.
I waked, not buried in pebbles

Behind the tank car,
But in the glimmering steeple
That sprang as I said it would
And lifted the young married couples,
Clutching their credit cards,
Boldly into and out of
Their American lives.
I said to myself that the poor
Would always be poor until
The towers I knew of should rise
And the oil be tapped:
That I had literally sung
My sick country up from its deathbed,
But nothing would do,
No logical right holds the truth.
In the sealed rooms I think of this,
Recording the nursery songs
In a checkered and tailored shirt,

As a guest on TV shows
And in my apartment now:
This is all a thing I began
To believe, to change, and to sell
When I opened my mouth to the rich.

PART THREE

THE BEING

I

It is there, above him, beyond, behind,

Distant, and near where he lies in his sleep
Bound down as for warranted torture.
Through his eyelids he sees it

Drop off its wings or its clothes.
He groans, and breaks almost from

Or into another sleep.
Something fills the bed he has been
Able only to half-fill.

He turns and buries his head.

II

Moving down his back,
Back up his back,
Is an infinite, unworldly frankness,
Showing him what an entire

143

Possession nakedness is.
Something over him

Is praying.
                    It reaches down under
His eyelids and gently lifts them.
He expects to look straight into eyes
And to see thereby through the roof.

III

Darkness. The windowpane stirs.
His lids close again, and the room

Begins to breathe on him
As through the eyeholes of a mask.

The praying of prayer
Is not in the words but the breath.

It sees him and touches him
All over, from everywhere.
It lifts him from the mattress
To be able to flow around him

In the heat from a coal bed burning
Far under the earth.
He enters — enters with . . .

What? His tongue? A word?
His own breath? Some part of his body?
All.
                            None.

He lies laughing silently
In the dark of utter delight.

IV

It glides, glides
Lightly over him, over his chest and legs.
All breath is called suddenly back

Out of laughter and weeping at once.
His face liquefies and freezes

Like a mask. He goes rigid
And breaks into sweat from his heart
All over his body

In something's hands.

V

He sleeps, and the windowpane
Ceases to flutter.
Frost crawls down off it
And backs into only
The bottom two corners of glass.

VI

He stirs, with the sun held at him
Out of late-winter dawn, and blazing
Levelly into his face.
He blazes back with his eyes closed,
Given, also, renewed

Fertility, to raise
Dead plants and half-dead beasts

145

Out of their thawing holes,

And children up,
From mortal women or angels,
As true to themselves as he

Is only in visited darkness
For one night out of the year,

And as he is now, seeing straight
Through the roof   wide   wider

Wide awake.

BREATH

Breath is on my face when the cloudy sun
  Is on my neck.
By it, the dangers of water are carefully
  Kept; kept back:

This is done with your father again
  In memory, it says.
Let me kneel on the boards of the rowboat,
  Father, where it sways

Among the fins and shovel heads
  Of surfaced sharks
And remember how I saw come shaping up
  Through lightening darks

Of the bay another thing that rose
  From the depths on air
And opened the green of its skull to breathe
  What we breathed there.

A porpoise circled around where I
  Lay in your hands
And felt my fear apportioned to the sharks,
  Which fell to sands

Two hundred feet down within cold.
  Looking over the side,
I saw that beak rise up beneath my face
  And a hole in the head

Open greenly, and then show living pink,
  And breath come out

In a mild, unhurried, unfathomable sigh
        That raised the boat

    And left us all but singing in midair.
        Have you not seen,
Father, in Heaven, the eye of earthly things
        Open and breathe green,

    Bestowing comfort on the mortal soul
        In deadly doubt,
Sustaining the spirit moving on the waters
        In hopeless light?

    We arched and plunged with that beast to land.
        Amazing, that unsealed lung
Come up from the dark; that breath, controlled,
        Greater than song,

    That huge body raised from the sea
        Secretly smiling
And shaped by the air it had carried
        Through the stark sailing

    And changeless ignorance of brutes,
        So that a dream
Began in my closed head, of the curves and rolling
        Powers of seraphim,

    That lift the good man's coffin on their breath
        And bear it up,
A rowboat, from the sons' depleting grief
        That will not stop:

Those that hide within time till the time
     Is wholly right,
Then come to us slowly, out of nowhere and anywhere risen,
     Breathlessly bright.

THE ICE SKIN

All things that go deep enough
Into rain and cold
Take on, before they break down,
A shining in every part.
The necks of slender trees
Reel under it, too much crowned,
Like princes dressing as kings,

And the redwoods let sink their branches
Like arms that try to hold buckets
Filling slowly with diamonds

Until a cannon goes off
Somewhere inside the still trunk
And a limb breaks, just before midnight,
Plunging houses into the darkness
And hands into cupboards, all seeking
Candles, and finding each other.
There is this skin

Always waiting in cold-enough air.
I have seen aircraft, in war,
Squatting on runways,

Dazed with their own enclosed,
Coming-forth, intensified color
As though seen by a child in a poem.
I have felt growing over
Me in the heated death rooms
Of uncles, the ice
Skin, that which the dying

Lose, and we others,
In their thawing presence, take on.
I have felt the heroic glaze

Also, in hospital waiting
Rooms: that masterly shining
And the slow weight that makes you sit
Like an emperor, fallen, becoming
His monument, with the stiff thorns
Of fear upside down on the brow,
An overturned kingdom:

Through the window of ice
I have stared at my son in his cage,
Just born, just born.

I touched the frost of my eyebrows
To the cold he turned to
Blindly, but sensing a thing.
Neither glass nor the jagged
Helm on my forehead would melt.
My son now stands with his head
At my shoulder. I

Stand, stooping more, but the same,
Not knowing whether
I will break before I can feel,

Before I can give up my powers,
Or whether the ice light
In my eyes will ever snap off
Before I die. I am still,

And my son, doing what he was taught,
Listening hard for a buried cannon,
Stands also, calm as glass.

BUMS, ON WAKING

Bums, on waking,
Do not always find themselves
In gutters with water running over their legs
And the pillow of the curbstone
Turning hard as sleep drains from it.
Mostly, they do not know

But hope for where they shall come to.
The opening of the eye is precious,

And the shape of the body also,
Lying as it has fallen,
Disdainfully crumpling earthward
Out of alcohol.
Drunken under their eyelids
Like children sleeping toward Christmas,

They wait for the light to shine
Wherever it may decide.

Often it brings them staring
Through glass in the rich part of town,
Where the forms of humanized wax
Are arrested in midstride
With their heads turned, and dressed
By force. This is ordinary, and has come

To be disappointing.
They expect and hope for

Something totally other:
That while they staggered last night

For hours, they got clear,
Somehow, of the city; that they
Have burst through a hedge, and are lying
In a trampled rose garden,

Pillowed on a bulldog's side,
A watchdog's, whose breathing

Is like the earth's, unforced —
Or that they may, once a year
(Any dawn now), awaken
In church, not on the coffin boards
Of a back pew, or on furnace-room rags,
But on the steps of the altar

Where candles are opening their eyes
With all-seeing light

And the green stained glass of the windows
Falls on them like sanctified leaves.
Who else has quite the same
Commitment to not being sure
What he shall behold, come from sleep —
A child, a policeman, an effigy?

Who else has died and thus risen?
Never knowing how they have got there,

They might just as well have walked
On water, through walls, out of graves,
Through potter's fields and through barns,
Through slums where their stony pillows

Refused to harden, because of
Their hope for this morning's first light,

With water moving over their legs
More like living cover than it is.

GOODBYE TO SERPENTS

Through rain falling on us no faster
Than it runs down the wall we go through,
My son and I shed Paris like a skin
And slip into a cage to say goodbye.
Through a hole in the wall
Of the Jardin des Plantes
We come to go round

The animals for the last time;
Tomorrow we set out for home.
For some reason it is the snakes
To which we seem to owe
The longest farewell of our lives.
These have no bars, but drift
On an island held still by a moat,

Unobstructedly gazing out.
My son will not move from watching
Them through the dust of cold water,
And neither will I, when I realize
That this is my farewell
To Europe also. I begin to look
More intently than I ever have.

In the moat one is easily swimming
Like the essence of swimming itself,
Pure line and confident curve
Requiring no arms or legs.
In a tree, a bush, there is one
Whose body is living there motionless,
Emotionless, with drops running down,

His slack tail holding a small
Growing gem that will not fall.
I can see one's eyes in the brush,
As fixed as a portrait's,
Gazing into, discovering, forgetting
The heart of all rainfall and sorrow.
He licks at the air,

Tasting the carded water
Changed by the leaves of his home.
The rain stops in midair before him
Mesmerized as a bird—
A harmony of drops in which I see
Towers and churches, domes,
Capitals, streets like the shining

Paths of the Jardin des Plantes,
All old, all cold with my gaze
In glittering, unearthly fascination.
I say, "Yes! So I have seen them!
But I have brought also the human,
The presence of self and of love."
Yet it is not so. My son shifts

Uneasily back and away, bored now,
A tourist to the bitter end,
And I know I have not been moved
Enough by the things I have moved through,
And I have seen what I have seen

Unchanged, hypnotized, and perceptive:
The jewelled branches,

The chandeliers, the windows
Made for looking through only when weeping,
The continent hazy with grief,
The water in the air without support
Sustained in the serpent's eye.

IN THE CHILD'S NIGHT

On distant sides of the bed
We lie together in the winter house
Trying to go away.

Something thinks, "You must be made for it,
And tune your quiet body like a fish
To the stars of the Milky Way

To pass into the star-sea, into sleep,
By means of the heart of the current,
The holy secret of flowing."

Yet levels of depth are wrestling
And rising from us; we are still.
The quilt pattern — a child's pink whale —

Has surfaced through ice at midnight
And now is dancing upon
The dead cold and middle of the air

On my son's feet:
His short legs are trampling the bedclothes
Into the darkness above us

Where the chill of consciousness broods
Like a thing of absolute evil.
I rise to do freezing battle

With my bare hands.
I enter the faraway other
Side of the struggling bed

And turn him to face me.
The stitched beast falls, and we
Are sewn warmly into a sea-shroud

It begins to haul through the dark.
Holding my son's
Best kicking foot in my hand,

I begin to move with the moon
As it must have felt when it went
From the sea to dwell in the sky,

As we near the vast beginning,
The unborn stars of the wellhead,
The secret of the game.

APPROACHING PRAYER

A moment tries to come in
Through the windows, when one must go
Beyond what there is in the room,

But it must come straight down.
Lord, it is time,

And I must get up and start
To circle through my father's empty house
Looking for things to put on
Or to strip myself of
So that I can fall to my knees
And produce a word I can't say
Until all my reason is slain.

Here is the gray sweater
My father wore in the cold,
The snapped threads growing all over it
Like his gray body hair.
The spurs of his gamecocks glimmer
Also, in my light, dry hand.
And here is the head of a boar
I once helped to kill with two arrows:

Two things of my father's
Wild, Bible-reading life
And my own best and stillest moment
In a hog's head waiting for glory.

All these I set up in the attic,
The boar's head, gaffs, and the sweater

On a chair, and gaze in the dark
Up into the boar's painted gullet.

Nothing. Perhaps I should feel more foolish,
Even, than this.
I put on the ravelled nerves

And gray hairs of my tall father
In the dry grave growing like fleece,
Strap his bird spurs to my heels
And kneel down under the skylight.
I put on the hollow hog's head
Gazing straight up
With star points in the glass eyes
That would blind anything that looked in

And cause it to utter words.
The night sky fills with a light

Of hunting: with leaves
And sweat and the panting of dogs

Where one tries hard to draw breath,
A single breath, and hold it.
I draw the breath of life
For the dead hog:
I catch it from the still air,
Hold it in the boar's rigid mouth,
And see

A young aging man with a bow
And a green arrow pulled to his cheek
Standing deep in a mountain creek bed,
Stiller than trees or stones,
Waiting and staring

Beasts, angels,
I am nearly that motionless now

There is a frantic leaping at my sides
Of dogs coming out of the water

The moon and the stars do not move

I bare my teeth, and my mouth
Opens, a foot long, popping with tushes

A word goes through my closed lips

I gore a dog, he falls, falls back
Still snapping, turns away and dies
While swimming. I feel each hair on my back
Stand up through the eye of a needle

Where the hair was
On my head stands up
As if it were there

The man is still; he is stiller: still

Yes.

Something comes out of him
Like a shaft of sunlight or starlight.
I go forward toward him

(Beasts, angels)

With light standing through me,
Covered with dogs, but the water
Tilts to the sound of the bowstring

The planets attune all their orbits

The sound from his fingers,
Like a plucked word, quickly pierces
Me again, the trees try to dance
Clumsily out of the wood

I have said something else

And underneath, underwater,
In the creek bed are dancing
The sleepy pebbles

The universe is creaking like boards
Thumping with heartbeats
And bonebeats

And every image of death
In my head turns red with blood.
The man of blood does not move

My father is pale on my body

> The dogs of blood
> Hang to my ears,
> The shadowy bones of the limbs
> The sun lays on the water
> Mass darkly together

Moonlight, moonlight

> The sun mounts my hackles
> And I fall; I roll
> In the water;
> My tongue spills blood
> Bound for the ocean;
> It moves away, and I see
> The trees strain and part, see him
> Look upward

Inside the hair helmet
I look upward out of the total
Stillness of killing with arrows.
I have seen the hog see me kill him
And I was as still as I hoped.
I am that still now, and now.
My father's sweater
Swarms over me in the dark.
I see nothing, but for a second

Something goes through me
Like an accident, a negligent glance,

Like the explosion of a star
Six billion light years off
Whose light gives out

Just as it goes straight through me.
The boar's blood is sailing through rivers
Bearing the living image
Of my most murderous stillness.
It picks up speed
And my heart pounds.
The chicken-blood rust at my heels
Freshens, as though near a death wound
Or flight. I nearly lift
From the floor, from my father's grave
Crawling over my chest,

And then get up
In the way I usually do.
I take off the head of the hog
And the gaffs and the panting sweater
And go down the dusty stairs
And never come back.

I don't know quite what has happened
Or that anything has,

Hoping only that
The irrelevancies one thinks of
When trying to pray
Are the prayer,

And that I have got by my own
Means to the hovering place
Where I can say with any
Other than the desert fathers —
Those who saw angels come,
Their body glow shining on bushes
And sheep's wool and animal eyes,
To answer what questions men asked
In Heaven's tongue,
Using images of earth
Almightily:

PROPHECIES, FIRE IN THE SINFUL TOWERS,
WASTE AND FRUITION IN THE LAND,
CORN, LOCUSTS AND ASHES,
THE LION'S SKULL PULSING WITH HONEY,
THE BLOOD OF THE FIRST-BORN,
A GIRL MADE PREGNANT WITH A GLANCE
LIKE AN EXPLODING STAR
AND A CHILD BORN OF UTTER LIGHT —

Where I can say only, and truly,
That my stillness was violent enough,
That my brain had blood enough,
That my right hand was steady enough,
That the warmth of my father's wool grave
Imparted love enough
And the keen heels of feathery slaughter
Provided lift enough,
That reason was dead enough

For something important to be:

That, if not heard,
It may have been somehow said.

PART FOUR

THE DRIVER

At the end of the war I arose
From my bed in the tent and walked
Where the island fell through white stones
Until it became the green sea.
Into light that dazzled my brain
Like the new thought of peace, I walked
Until I was swimming and singing.

Over the foundered landing craft
That took the island, I floated,
And then like a thistle came
On the deep wind of water to rest
Far out, my long legs of shadow down-
pointing to ground where my soul
Could take root and spring as it must.

Below me a rusted halftrack
Moved in the depths with the movement
One sees a thing take through tears
Of joy, or terrible sorrow,

A thing which in quietness lies
Beyond both. Slowly I sank
And slid into the driver's shattered seat.

Driving through the country of the drowned
On a sealed, secret-keeping breath,
Ten feet under water, I sat still,
Getting used to the burning stare
Of the wide-eyed dead after battle.
I saw, through the sensitive roof —
The uneasy, lyrical skin that lies

Between death and life, trembling always —
An airplane come over, perfectly
Soundless, but could not tell
Why I lived, or why I was sitting,
With my lungs being shaped like two bells,
At the wheel of a craft in a wave
Of attack that broke upon coral.

"I become pure spirit," I tried
To say, in a bright smoke of bubbles,
But I was becoming no more
Than haunted, for to be so
Is to sink out of sight, and to lose
The power of speech in the presence
Of the dead, with the eyes turning green,

And to leap at last for the sky
Very nearly too late, where another
Leapt and could not break into
His breath, where it lay, in battle

As in peace, available, secret,
Dazzling and huge, filled with sunlight,
For thousands of miles on the water.

HORSES AND PRISONERS

In the war where many men fell
Wind blew in a ring, and was grass.
Many horses fell also to rifles
On a track in the Philippine Islands
And divided their still, wiry meat
To be eaten by prisoners.
I sat at the finish line
At the end of the war

Knowing that I would live.
Long grass went around me, half wind,
Where I rode the rail of the infield
And the dead horses travelled in waves
On past the finishing post.
Dead wind lay down in live grass,
The flowers, pounding like hooves,
Stood up in the sun and were still,

And my mind, like a fence on fire,
Went around those unknown men:
Those who tore from the red, light bones
The intensified meat of hunger
And then lay down open-eyed
In a raw, straining dream of new life.
Joy entered the truth and flowed over
As the wind rose out of the grass

Leaping with red and white flowers:
Joy in the bone-strewn infield
Where clouds of barbed wire contained
Men who ran in a vision of greenness,
Sustained by the death of beasts,

On the tips of the sensitive grass blades,
Each footstep putting forth petals,
Their bones light and strong as the wind.

From the fence I dropped off and waded
Knee-deep in the billowing homestretch
And picked up the red of one flower.
It beat in my hand like my heart,
Filled with the pulse of the air,
And I felt my long thighbones yearn
To leap with the trained, racing dead.
When beasts are fallen in wars

For food, men seeking a reason to live
Stand mired in the on-going grass
And sway there, sweating and thinking,
With fire coming out of their brains
Like the thought of food and life
Of prisoners. When death moves close
In the night, I think I can kill it:
Let a man let his mind burn and change him

To one who was prisoner here
As he sings in his sleep in his home,
His mane streaming over the pillows,
The white threads of time
Mixed with the hair of his temples,
His grave-grass risen without him:
Now, in the green of that sleep,
Let him start the air of the island

From the tangled gate of jute string
That hangs from the battered grandstand
Where hope comes from animal blood
And the hooves of ghosts become flowers
That a captive may run as in Heaven:
Let him strip the dead shirt from his chest
And, sighing like all saved men,
Take his nude child in his arms.

DRINKING FROM A HELMET

I

I climbed out, tired of waiting
For my foxhole to turn in the earth
On its side or its back for a grave,
And got in line
Somewhere in the roaring of dust.
Every tree on the island was nowhere,
Blasted away.

II

In the middle of combat, a graveyard
Was advancing after the troops
With laths and balls of string;
Grass already tinged it with order.
Between the new graves and the foxholes
A green water-truck stalled out.
I moved up on it, behind
The hill that cut off the firing.

III

My turn, and I shoved forward
A helmet I picked from the ground,
Not daring to take mine off
Where somebody else may have come
Loose from the steel of his head.

IV

Keeping the foxhole doubled
In my body and begging
For water, safety, and air,
I drew water out of the truckside
As if dreaming the helmet full.

In my hands, the sun
Came on in a feathery light.

V

In midair, water trimming
To my skinny dog-faced look
Showed my life's first all-out beard
Growing wildly, escaping from childhood,
Like the beards of the dead, all now
Underfoot beginning to grow.
Selected ripples wove through it,
Knocked loose with a touch from all sides
Of a brain killed early that morning,
Most likely, and now
In its absence holding
My sealed, sunny image from harm,
Weighing down my hands,
Shipping at the edges,
Too heavy on one side, then the other.

VI

I drank, with the timing of rust.
A vast military wedding
Somewhere advanced one step.

VII

All around, equipment drifting in light,
Men drinking like cattle and bushes,
Cans, leather, canvas and rifles,
Grass pouring down from the sun
And up from the ground.

176

Grass: and the summer advances
Invisibly into the tropics.
Wind, and the summer shivers
Through many men standing or lying
In the GI gardener's hand
Spreading and turning green
All over the hill.

VIII

At the middle of water
Bright circles dawned inward and outward
Like oak rings surviving the tree
As its soul, or like
The concentric gold spirit of time.
I kept trembling forward through something
Just born of me.

IX

My nearly dead power to pray
Like an army increased and assembled,
As when, in a harvest of sparks,
The helmet leapt from the furnace
And clamped itself
On the heads of a billion men.
Some words directed to Heaven
Went through all the strings of the graveyard
Like a message that someone sneaked in,
Tapping a telegraph key
At dead of night, then running
For his life.

X

I swayed, as if kissed in the brain.
Above the shelled palm-stumps I saw
How the tops of huge trees might be moved
In a place in my own country
I never had seen in my life.
In the closed dazzle of my mouth
I fought with a word in the water
To call on the dead to strain
Their muscles to get up and go there.
I felt the difference between
Sweat and tears when they rise,
Both trying to melt the brow down.

On even the first day of death
The dead cannot rise up,
But their last thought hovers somewhere
For whoever finds it.
My uninjured face floated strangely
In the rings of a bodiless tree.
Among them, also, a final
Idea lived, waiting
As in Ariel's limbed, growing jail.

I stood as though I possessed
A cool, trembling man
Exactly my size, swallowed whole.
Leather swung at his waist,
Web-cord, buckles, and metal,
Crouching over the dead

Where they waited for all their hands
To be connected like grass-roots.

XIII

In the brown half-life of my beard
The hair stood up
Like the awed hair lifting the back
Of a dog that has eaten a swan.
Now light like this
Staring into my face
Was the first thing around me at birth.
Be no more killed, it said.

XIV

The wind in the grass
Moved gently in secret flocks,
Then spread to be
Nothing, just where they were.
In delight's
Whole shining condition and risk,
I could see how my body might come
To be imagined by something
That thought of it only for joy.

XV

Fresh sweat and unbearable tears
Drawn up by my feet from the field
Between my eyebrows became
One thing at last,
And I could cry without hiding.
The world dissolved into gold;
I could have stepped up into air.

I drank and finished
Like tasting of Heaven,
Which is simply of,
At seventeen years,
Not dying wherever you are.

XVI

Enough
Shining, I picked up my carbine and said.
I threw my old helmet down
And put the wet one on.
Warmed water ran over my face.
My last thought changed, and I knew
I inherited one of the dead.

XVII

I saw tremendous trees
That would grow on the sun if they could,
Towering. I saw a fence
And two boys facing each other,
Quietly talking,
Looking in at the gigantic redwoods,
The rings in the trunks turning slowly
To raise up stupendous green.
They went away, one turning
The wheels of a blue bicycle,
The smaller one curled catercornered
In the handlebar basket.

XVIII

I would survive and go there,
Stepping off the train in a helmet

That held a man's last thought,
Which showed him his older brother
Showing him trees.
I would ride through all
California upon two wheels
Until I came to the white
Dirt road where they had been,
Hoping to meet his blond brother,
And to walk with him into the wood
Until we were lost,
Then take off the helmet
And tell him where I had stood,
What poured, what spilled, what swallowed:

XIX
And tell him I was the man.

ABOUT THE AUTHOR

JAMES DICKEY is a former night-fighter pilot with more than 100 missions in World War II, an athlete, hunter, and woodsman, and author of the novel and screenplay *Deliverance*. Now Poet in Residence and Carolina Professor at the University of South Carolina, he has also taught at Rice University, Reed College, the University of Wisconsin, and the University of Florida. He has been twice appointed Poetry Consultant to the Library of Congress and in 1977 read a poem written in honor of former President Carter at the Inaugural Concert Gala. He lives in Columbia, South Carolina.